Is He Mr. Right?

How To Tell If You Should LOVE HIM or LEAVE HIM...

...The Many Ways He Reveals His Hidden Love Codes

DAVID A. SAMSON
www.funnyguy.com

ELAYNE J. KAHN, PhD.
www.lovecodes.com

by the authors of *Is He For Real?*

Is He Mr. Right?: How To Tell If You Should LOVE HIM or LEAVE HIM...

For further information, contact:

S.P.I. Books
99 Spring Street, 3rd Floor
New York, NY 10012
Tel: (212) 431-5011
Fax: (212) 431-8646
E-mail: publicity@spibooks.com

10 9 8 7 6 5 4 3 2 1
First Edition

Library of Congress Cataloging-in-Publication Data available.

S.P.I. Books World Wide Web address: *www.spibooks.com*

ISBN: 1-56171-912-9

DEDICATED TO

The loving memory of Mollie Rudnitsky.
Truly, an Angel on Earth.

and

Judi Kahn Pitkowsky.
Who has been there for everyone.
Always with joy and goodwill.
Always with unconditional love.

MORE BOOKS BY
DAVID A. SAMSON and ELAYNE J. KAHN

- **Is He For Real?** *Knowing Sooner What A Men Will Be Like Later* **(SPI Books)**
- **1001 Ways You Reveal Your Personality**
- **1001 More Ways You Reveal Your Personality**
- **Parents Who Stay Lovers**
- **Love Codes**

EVEN MORE BOOKS BY DAVID A. SAMSON

- **The Joy of Depression (SPI Books)**
- **Do Reality Checks Ever Bounce? (SPI Books)**
- **The ANTI-Motivation Handbook**
- **Men Who Hate Themselves - And The Women Who Agree With Them! (SPI Books)**
- **The Official Millennium Survival Handbook** (with Peter Bergman) **(SPI Books)**
- **Rob Parr's Post Pregnancy Workout** (with Rob Parr)
- **Tammy Faye: Telling It My Way** (with Tammy Faye Bakker)
- **The Book Of Useless Knowledge** (with Joe Edelman)

AND EVEN MORE BOOKS BY ELAYNE J. KAHN

- **The Whole Body Health and Sex Book** (with Gary Null)
- **The How To Feel Good Handbook**

CONTENTS

DAVID A. SAMSON

Mr. Samson (aka David A. Rudnitsky) is the author or co-author of twelve books. His books have appeared in over 20 countries from Brazil to Turkey, France to China. They Have been excerpted in hundreds of newspapers and magazines including *Cosmopolitan, Mademoiselle, Penthouse, Playboy, People, US, Self, Working Women, Seventeen, American Way, USA Today, The Entertainment Weekly, Newsday*, plus *The New York Times and London Times*.

What's more, they have been featured on *Oprah, Live With Regis & Kathy Lee, Geraldo Rivera, The Today Show,* ABC's *Prime Time, Rosie O'Donnell, The Fox Morning News, Comedy Central, Politically Incorrect, Hard Copy, Entertainment Tonight, David Letterman, Good Morning America*, and *Larry King Live*.

Mr. Samson is a much sought-after corporate speaker and consultant, an advertising and marketing expert, and a prestigious member of the National Speakers Association. He has been a Senior Creative Executive at some of America's most prestigious advertising agencies including Saatchi and Saatchi, Lantas Worlwide, Young & Rubicam, and McCann Erickson, but you better not ask him about it!

Mr. Samson divides his money between Beverly Hills and New York. He believes the best years of his life are still behind him.

*Visit him at: **www.funnyguy.com***

ELAYNE J. KAHN, Ph.D.

Dr. Kahn holds degree from Harvard University. For over a decade, she was Director of the New York Center for Sexual and Marital Guidance. She has been a clinical instructor at the City University of New York, Union Collage, and the School of Visual Arts (New York).

At Brookdale Hospital, Dr. Kahn was the Chief Psychologist of the comprehensive Childcare Unit. She has also been a clinical psychologist at the University of Virginia Medical Center, a psychological consultant to the New York City Board of Education, and has studied at the Master's and Johnson Institute in St. Louis.

Dr. Kahn wrote the *How to Feel Good Handbook* and co-authored *The Whole Body Sex and Health Book* with Gary Null. She has also co-written four other books with David Samson including *Is He For Real?, 1001 Ways You Reveal Your Personality, 1001 More Ways You Reveal Your Personality, Love Codes*, plus *Parents Who Stay Lovers*.

Her books have been excerpted or serialized in hundreds of newspapers and magazines including **People, Mademoiselle, Cosmopolitan, US, Self, Working Woman, Seventeen**, and **USA Today**. They've been translated around the world from Turkey to Brazil and even China. What's more, Dr. Kahn has been featured on numerous TV and radio interviews as well including **Donahue** and **Oprah**.

Currently, Dr, Kahn has an extensive private practice in Miami Beach specializing in interpersonal issues and relationships. She is listed in **Who's Who of American Women,** and her pioneering work continues to be internationally acclaimed.

Visit her at: **www.lovecodes.com**

INTRODUCTION

In our first book, *IS HE FOR REAL?*, you learned how to tell sooner what a man will be like later: the secrets of deciphering his secret signals of romance. Our first book revealed hundreds of Love Codes that could be used when you initially meet someone. The way they dress, what music they listen to, the way they tip, the way they drive, even what's in their medicine chest can all provide vital and intimate personal data.

But this definitive volume goes one step further. It boldly journeys into the most hidden regions of men's hearts—and more importantly, answers whether or not you should take him into your heart. Without a doubt, this book shows if he's emotionally honest and sexually mature or a mama's boy. It reveals how much love he's ready to give you—and how much he's holding back! For men betray their real attitudes about relationships in the most innocent ways, and these clues are everywhere, waiting to be deciphered by your discerning eye!

So therefore, now that you've been seeing him for awhile, the most important question becomes *IS HE MR. RIGHT?* Is he the right person for a long-term relationship or marriage? Is he the right man to be the father of your children, or be a good father to the children you already have? Is he emotionally stable and secure? Does he have true integrity? Is he a man who does what he says he will? Can he remain sexually stimulating and continue to adore you as a woman? Will he sustain a faithful relationship or cheat on you? Are there hidden warning signs that you should be aware of? Is he likely (somewhere down the line) to reject you without warning? Will he turn verbally cruel and perhaps physically abusive? Should you not get involved any further and start to back away? Or should you definitely embrace this man without reservation?

These are all questions that need to be answered before you go any deepen with this relationship. But fortunately, this book picks up precisely where our first book (*Is He For Real?*—S.P.I. Books) left off. It delves more deeply into his emotional scripts and makes more definitive predictions about your prospects with him. Bearing this in mind, it can also disclose how to spot a man who is ready for a meaningful relationship—even before he realizes it himself!

Most of the chapters call for astute observations of his day-to-day behavior, insights that can only be gotten after you've been with him for a period of time. Nevertheless, they're not difficult to decode. Just be aware they exist in every man, and that they can be interpreted with penetrating accuracy. Since this work is based on hundreds of case studies as well as psychological research, you now have a surefire method to eliminate any doubts which may still be lingering, such as:

- **Is he ready to commit—or should he be committed?**
- **Will he be reliable if the going gets rough—or flake out?**
- **Does he want to build a relationship—or to tear you down?**
- **Is he self-confident—or merely self-deluding?**
- **Does he need his space—or is he spaced out?**
- **And finally: Should you wed him—or shed him?**

In this handbook, we will analyze his actions from every possible angle. We will decipher his cultural messages, what his preferences really mean from sports to movies to art. We will uncover the hidden meanings behind his work performance or chosen profession and detail how that impacts the future of your personal relationship with him. In other words, will the cost of his success extract a high price from you? On top of that, we will show how to perceive his relationships with other people, the crucial and candid cues that are disclosed by the company he keeps.

As you gain faith in your powers of scrutiny, you will begin to interpret the way he acts at parties, openings, or other social events. You will watch his body language, actions, conversations, and other foolproof signals which divulge the person he truly is inside. Here, you will also master the tools you need to uncover the dynamics of his family relationships, the effect parents and siblings have had upon him, and ultimately the effect that this will have upon the two of you. As a matter of fact, you will even be able to gauge the effects of previous marriages and relationships upon his psyche, before any of his secret dramas turn out to have tragic results for your ongoing relationship.

On the sexual front, we will tell you what's actually going on—both in and outside of bed! From foreplay to everything that comes afterwards, this book will lay bare the reality behind the complex and often confusing signals which he may be sending out. Using the special data contained within, you can easily dissect his flirting behavior, kissing, and even lovemaking style. You can become instantly aware of his true desires and preferences, thereby learning of the pleasures (or pain) yet to be experienced with him.

Then again, because a strong sexual connection can lead to misleading conclusions, this book will help you determine if he has something as common as performance anxiety—or if he harbors deeper, darker fears about women. Is he in sexual denial or doubt? Or is he secretly intent on robbing you of your sensual self-esteem? All these concerns will be answered, and many more as well!

The bottom line is that if you're really serious about making a commitment to a man, this book will prove invaluable. By knowing a man's true character, it becomes easier to gain his trust and win him over. You can more easily distinguish those men who talk a good relationship, but never actually walk it. By measuring his true self against your own desires, you can accelerate the process of knowing whether or not the two of you are truly meant for each other. Undeniably, by gaining more insights into his nature, you can help avoid any serious pitfalls that could possibly wreak emotional havoc on you because of your involvement

When all is said and done, after evaluating a man using the data in this book, the surest predictor of a successful relationship boils down to eight key points:

THE 8 KEY POINTS TO A SUCCESSFUL RELATIONSHIP:

- **Mutual respect and acceptance**
- **Congruent goals and values**
- **Emotional compatibility**
- **Constructive openness and honesty**
- **Physical attraction and harmonious sexuality**
- **Shared interests and activities**
- **Expressions of affection**
- **Appreciation, realistic expectations.**

There's no doubt about it. The insightful approach described herein will give you the power to see through any man in just a few days. No more waiting months, even years, to find what really makes him tick—or that you've made a terrible mistake. Of course, selecting the perfect person is always a challenging task, but now you have a way to know his true colors for sure.

In the final analysis, we believe that being part of a couple provides a sense of security and well-being unmatched by any other human experience. Two people who bring out the best in each other can literally take on the world, as they create a joyous world of their own and inspire everyone else in their lives to reach the same level of contentment.

Is He Mr. Right? It would be wrong to let another minute go by without finding out!

CHAPTER • ONE

IS HE A PRODUCT
OF HIS CULTURE?

Art is an enigmatic blend of imagination, fantasy, and desire. A means of expression unfettered by conventional boundaries, art uses a variety of mediums to make statements that are at once emotional, sensual, and informational. A man's cultural preferences—from the books he reads to the art museums he frequents—reveal his deepest emotional and psychological beliefs, beliefs that have tremendous bearing on his attitudes about love and romance.

Clearly the man who appreciates the complexities of a Wagnerian opera is very different from someone turned on by Cyndi Lauper or Michael Jackson. He who is engrossed in the latest adventures of a Marvel Comic superhero has a very different outlook on the world than someone whose idea of light reading is a six-volume set on Roman civilization. Cultural preferences can be much more complex or much more subtle, of course. What of the man whose eclectic musical tastes run from arrhythmic jazz to forties show tunes? Or the fellow who never sees a film unless it has subtitles, but has a hidden weakness for "Three's Company"?

Carefully observe your man's tastes in books, music, and film if you want a revealing portrait of what he is *really* like.

Deciphering Cultural Messages

1. When you consider his preferences in art, books, television, theater, or film, do you find that he:
   a. Is fond of one particular subject or theme?
   b. Appreciates a variety of styles and approaches?
   c. Tends to have tastes that are unusual?

2. What sort of entertainment does he seek out?
   a. Light, escapist fare.
   b. Cultural activities laden with social messages.
   c. A combination of both.

3. In terms of his cultural preferences, is he:
   a. Open to new experiences?
   b. Rigid and inflexible?
   c. Strong, but willing to be swayed on occasion?

4. After seeing a performance together, does he:
   a. Insist on delivering critical lectures, as if you lacked his intellectual range?
   b. Enjoy analyzing and discussing the event?
   c. Often agree with your opinion without adding insights of his own?

5. What are his reading habits?
   a. He consumes books and magazines voraciously.
   b. His reading is confined mostly to the newspaper.
   c. He reads books and magazines only in his field of interest.

6. *How much television does he watch?*
   a. More than three hours a night.
   b. About an hour a night.
   c. Very little, except for special programming.

7. *What is his record, tape, and compact disc collection like?*
   a. A collection of top-40 albums.
   b. An eclectic collection of jazz, classical, and theatrical music.
   c. A treasure trove of rare, outdated, or hard-to-find contemporary musical works.

8. *How does he respond to a performance he has just seen?*
   a. Implies that he could have done a better job himself.
   b. Assesses both its negative and positive dimensions.
   c. Offers little opinion one way or the other.

9. *Does he feel that:*
   a. Today's artists will never match the Old Masters?
   b. The contemporary art scene is dynamic and superior to the works of the past?
   c. That there have been great artists throughout history and will surely be others to come?

10. *Before deciding to see a new show, does he:*
    a. Wait to see what the critics have to say?
    b. Rely on the opinion of friends?
    c. Go and decide for himself?

The Score

Add up the points for each question and check the following answers:

1. a - 2
   b - 6
   c - 4

2. a - 2
   b - 4
   c - 6

3. a - 6
   b - 2
   c - 4

4. a - 4
   b - 6
   c - 2

5. a - 6
   b - 2
   c - 4

6. a - 2
   b - 4
   c - 6

7. a - 2
   b - 6
   c - 4

8. a - 4
   b - 6
   c - 2

9. a - 4
   b - 2
   c - 6

10. a - 4
    b - 2
    c - 6

[51–60 points]

This is a man of extraordinarily good taste and excellent critical judgment. The aesthetic dimensions of interpersonal relationships are very important to him, and he seeks women who share his openness to a wide range of cultural influences. He expects sophistication and astute judgment from a lover, but if you are as well-informed as he is, you will find him receptive to your evaluations and suggestions.

[41–50 points]

This man also has refined tastes and a certain finesse, but he holds stubbornly to certain beliefs and preferences. In general, you will find that he is well-informed, emotionally receptive, and reliable. His attitudes toward relationships are like his cultural judgments—generally pretty good but occasionally totally unreasonable. When he stops being reasonable, you must have the confidence to assert your own point of view.

[31–40 points]

From a cultural perspective, this man is neither fish nor fowl. Although he is an expert in some cultural arenas, he knows absolutely nothing about others, yet harbors the illusion that he does. If you become involved in a relationship with this man, you will find it difficult to sway him on certain matters, which can be extremely frustrating.

[20–30 points]

Better look elsewhere if you are seeking a man who is cultivated and elegant in his tastes. This man's sense of aesthetics is determined more by popular whim than by a refined ability to make critical judgments. On the plus side, however, is the fact that this is an easygoing man whose rather lax standards will not be difficult to meet.

You Can Make Book on It

Most book collections hold a treasure trove of clues about a man's beliefs, ideas, and values. The subject matter of the volumes, the way in which they are organized, and whether they have a well-thumbed or scant-read appearance reveal the nature of his intellectual and cultural interests. More important, careful extrapolation tells you what type of a lover your bookworm will make.

SHAWN: A POETIC EXPERIENCE

Maryanne: As soon as I walked into Shawn's apartment I noticed all the volumes of poetry he had. Our first evening together was almost an ethereal experience. He lit candles and read me poems in a rich, mellifluous voice that I found hypnotic. At the end of the evening, I stroked him gently as I said good night and was startled when he shuddered and withdrew his arm.

I went back to his apartment a few more times after that, but he never made the slightest effort to be physically affectionate. And I began to notice some other curious things that I had missed before—his volumes of poetry were arranged in strict alphabetical order, for example.

Maryanne was initially attracted to Shawn's intense and seemingly passionate nature. Unfortunately, her hopes that he would sweep her off her feet were quickly dashed. Shawn spent his emotional energy on his poetry and had little left to share with a living, breathing woman. He could speak about the passions of the soul but felt ill-at-ease with passions of the flesh.

On closer analysis, the clues to Shawn's rigid behavior were everywhere. The way in which he arranged his poetry suggests a man whose aesthetic preferences take second fiddle to a passion for orderliness. Perhaps his tightly proscribed habits made it easier for him to control an emotional life that threatened to overwhelm him; regardless, he could not loosen up enough to appreciate Maryanne's more casual and freewheeling spirit.

Are His Books Arranged in a Novel Way?

Whether a man arranges his books in a fastidious manner or totally haphazardly reveals something about his interest in reading and even more about his approach to loving.

First Things First

Often people put the books that are most significant to them within the easiest reach, at the center of the bookcase. They provide insight into your man's past and give you a sense of his priorities.

As you move away from that focal point, the books wane in importance, representing more superficial interests and attitudes. Pay attention to the books on the periphery. They just might hold a clue about a difficult-to-observe aspect of his personality that could drive you to distraction—or send you to the heights of euphoria.

The Subject Counts

Another systematic approach is to arrange books by subject. The sign of a true reader who likes to be able to find specific books easily, this man, too, takes good care of possessions that are important to him. A good sign because he is the kind of man who will transfer such a caring approach to you.

Aesthetic Appeal

Odder than either an alphabetical or a subject matter arrangement is an arrangement by height. In one library, a man's books were evenly aligned so that each shelf maintained a level effect. The priority for this man is form, not content. A man who uses books for aesthetic effect chooses women superficially, too, and is often more concerned about how they look than how they think.

Without Rhyme or Reason

When you enter his house, the first thing you see are books piled everywhere. Although you may have stumbled across an exceptionally well-read intellectual, you also may be dealing with a man whose mind is in great disarray. Although an individual like this can be very loving, he is likely to forget those special occasions, such as birthdays and anniversaries, that mean so much to you.

Does He Get Hard or Soft?

Hardcover

If hardcover volumes dominate his collection, you may have found a person who puts a high value on permanence. He values things that last, a trait that extends to his relationships, but he is highly critical and will dismiss a woman whom he judges frivolous.

Softcover

The man who collects mostly softcovers is a more adaptable personality. Contemporary in outlook and unlikely to get caught up in long-winded philosophical arguments, the paperback reader is less concerned with appearances, but may be very interested in substance.

Categorically Speaking

Study your man's book collection—and, most important, note the books that he is currently reading. If one category dominates his library, there is much that can be predicted about his behavior in a relationship. Here are some of the Love Codes those categories reveal.

Professional and Business

A preponderance of career-oriented and investment books indicates a successful man—or one determined to become successful. The fact that he thoroughly researches his subject before making a career move or risking his capital suggests that he is sensible and cautious enough not to fall for get-rich-quick schemes. Similarly, he may need time before he decides that you're a good investment. The only drawback to this go-getter is that he may be too obsessed with his career to make a relationship with you his top priority.

Self-Help Psychology

A person who avidly reads self-help books is open to change and interested in learning more about himself in order to improve. Someone who makes personal growth a priority is likely to seek a companion who also makes self-improvement a priority. Rather than sweeping problems in your relationship under the rug, such a man keeps all channels of communication open. Be on the lookout, however, for the individual who picks up every new pop psych book that appears on the market—he may be a bit *too* analytical and overly self-involved.

Classics

A man who reads the classics of great literature is generally well-educated, either through formal schooling or self-education, and has cultivated the ability to reason, to think things through, and to solve problems. Those attributes bode well for his ability to tackle the inevitable frictions of a relationship, although his style is overly intellectual for many.

Detective Novels

A devotee of Sherlock Holmes, Agatha Christie, or Raymond Chandler is generally good at noticing the details others might miss and enjoys exercising skills of logic and reasoning. Becoming involved with such a man could be intriguing, but beware of his strong streak of self-reliance—he may be reluctant to share *all* the intricacies of his life and may often keep you guessing.

Historical Novels

Whether it is a historical novel or books on military history, this man is fascinated with the past. He'll want to know all about your previous relationships and may irk you with his notion that history repeats itself. Such men are perceptive, though, and often draw intriguing connections between the isolated events of your past. You will also find him particularly forgiving and willing to over-look passing irritations.

Technical Manuals

A man whose bookshelves are lined with volumes about ma-chinery, cars, computers, and mathematics is logical and precise. He is more comfortable with the predictable behavior of machines than with the gray netherworld of emotions, although he may appreciate music and art with a passion. Often men with a technical bent are not emotionally demonstrative, so don't expect to be swept off your feet by this person.

A Multifaceted Collection

A person whose books cover many different topics is usually curious about life's many facets. Such curiosity often spawns maturity, tolerance, and a sophisticated outlook that translates into the flexibility required for a good relationship. A widely-read man has a broad perspective on the world, and his diverse interests make him a complex and intriguing partner.

RON: WHERE'S THE BEEF?

Joan: I was impressed by Ron's collection of high-priced art books, which are prominently displayed in his foyer. A beautifully bound set of Shakespearean plays in the hallway caught my eye. There was a small collection of rare books and rows of hardcovers, all in excellent condition. I thought to myself, "at last, a refined and cultured man." But when I mentioned how much I admired some of the classical writers, he looked as if he'd never heard their names before and seemed to know little about his own collection.

Here is a man who uses his books to convey an image, rather than to advance his store of knowledge. Appearance, rather than substance, is the force that drives him, a sign that he is deeply insecure and preoccupied with what others think of him. A man who judges books by their cover is likely to apply those same standards to women. Ron can fall madly in love with someone who projects the right image, then quickly grow disenchanted when he discovers her flaws. Only a woman who is equally concerned about image will be satisfied with such a self-centered man.

Music Is the Key

Music has been called the language of the gods. It is indeed a universal language, but its many dialects express a tremendously varied spectrum of moods and emotions. No one type of music is better or worse than another type, but the sounds a man prefers—and the way in which he listens to those sounds—show important personality traits. Learn how the Love Codes of a man captivated by free-spirited improvisational jazz contrast with those of the classical music devotee, for example, and you will be better able to identify *your* type of guy.

BARRY: NOT MUSIC TO HER EARS

Diane: My ears were ringing as the "Who" blared incessantly inside Barry's apartment, but the sex between us was fast, furious, and tremendously exciting. After we had both climaxed, the music really began to get on my nerves. I asked him to lower the volume but he just ignored my suggestion.

The combination of music and sex had charged the air with energy and we were both too wired to sleep. But Barry didn't respond to my efforts at conversation; he just grooved to the music and held me tight. When I finally reached over to lower the stereo, he blew up at me. "I just can't deal with a chick who jabbers on when I'm getting into my music," he said.

Barry's capacity to be totally consumed by music initially attracted Diane until she realized that he used music to disconnect himself from others. His passion for music became a barrier behind which he felt safe. The only other way he was able to express himself was in bed, but he could not translate physical intimacy into emotional intimacy. Barry's remarks to Diane and his refusal

to turn down the music at her request also show an insensitivity to her feelings that makes a giving relationship impossible.

From Adagio to Allegro

Primitive percussion sounds intoxicate one man but leave another cold. The man who is moved almost to tears by the haunting melody of an oboe may be utterly indifferent to the power of an electronic bass. Does he have the "blues"? Maybe that's his outlook on relationships as well as music.

Check out his music collection and note whether the albums, tapes, and CD's reflect a fondness for a particular decade, balance contemporary music with older favorites, or mix a range of styles. Here are the Love Codes behind particular styles of music:

Classical

A man who appreciates the subtle art of classical music is sensitive to the potential of human achievement. His is a mature sensibility that also values other artistic expressions, such as great paintings, timeless novels, and gourmet cuisine. People attuned to the classics are more introspective and private than most, and invariably insist on substance along with style. Although your classical music lover may not be given to wild displays of affection, he has deep feelings and the intellect to verbalize them.

Rock

A rock music aficionado tends to be more energetic and freer in his lifestyle than most men. Young at heart, tuned into contemporary trends, and a tad hedonistic, he may turn to the lyrics of his favorite rock musicians to justify his attitudes toward sex, work, responsibility, and freedom. If you share this man's obsession with rock and roll, you may just find that you are on the same wavelength.

Folk Music

A hard-core group of sensitive folks out there is still concerned with social issues and passionately committed to improving the environment, eliminating nuclear weapons, and promoting human rights. They see music as a tool to help save the world and value the ideas contained in the lyrics. If you are a woman devoted to good causes, the folkie can be a splendid choice—he is sincere, comfortable with himself, and appreciative of an honest and open relationship. Don't expect great wealth, though. These men aren't driven by the kind of ambition that translates into overwhelming financial success.

Jazz

Jazz enthusiasts are an eclectic collection of nonconformists who defy ready analysis. Although the underlying structure of jazz requires well-disciplined thinking, the brilliance of the music relies on improvisation and experimentation. Independence, a sense of adventure, a resistance to repetitive patterns, and a determination to do things his way are his hallmarks.

Here is a multifaceted individual guaranteed to give the woman in his life a one-of-a-kind experience. But be prepared, however, for the ups and downs of his fascinating, contradictory character, which will always remain unpredictable and uncontrollable.

Opera

The finest opera is laden with pomp and ceremony, and the man who cultivates a taste for this high art form has great respect for tradition and values predictability and appropriateness. In all manner of personal conduct and social interaction, he proceeds with style and taste. Be forewarned: An opera lover expects perfection, but when he sees what he likes, his enthusiasm is boundless. If you can tolerate a certain rigidity of thought, this man can offer you tremendous emotional rewards.

Top 40

Basically a romantic and easygoing guy, this man does not like to engage in endless introspective dialogue about relationships, preferring to see them evolve at their own relaxed pace. He does, however, hold the rather romantic notion that love with the right person will solve just about all of life's problems. Unfortunately, this fantasy makes it easier for him to walk away instead of confronting and dealing with tensions between you.

Country and Western

Here's a man who is in love with love and committed to pursuing close relationships but not always very successful at it. He is capable of experiencing deep emotion and talks as honestly about

poverty, rejection, and hardship as he does about successful con-
quests and rewarding relationships. One of the real charms of the
country-western buff is that he is unself-conscious and willing to
act silly, yet never compromises his self-respect.

Blues

This man treats life as an emotional, rather than an intellectual,
experience. Warm and communicative, he empathizes with the
struggles of others, especially in the realm of romance. He is
melancholy, but not cynical, about love and is willing to take
emotional risks, even if there is a chance of being rejected.

Show Tunes

Romantic and sensitive, this man has a nostalgic feeling for by-
gone days and a rather corny way with words. But he deliberates
carefully before talking and means every word he says so you'd
better watch your own language and avoid speaking carelessly. In
a relationship the show-tune addict tends to be a bit overly emotional, and prone to dramatic bursts of emotion, but it is all in the
interest of staving off the familiar and the boring.

Gospel

Preoccupied with religious values, his faith plays a significant
part in his life and he seeks a woman who shares his religious
beliefs. If your faith is comparable to his, you will find him a

trustworthy and dedicated family man. But if your spiritual values differ significantly, a meaningful long-term relationship is unlikely to develop.

Is He a Work of Art?

The art a man admires and chooses to display on his walls contains information about his self-image and his perspective on the world. Whether it is a photograph, a reproduction, or an original painting, we select art because it strikes a responsive chord in us and somehow helps to communicate our view of the world. In order to determine the Love Codes buried in a man's choices, look around his home and try to determine the statement that each piece of art makes.

Questionnaire: The Curator of the House

Answer each of the following questions with: All, Many, Some, Few, or None.

1. Does he display portraits of family and friends?

2. Are there sexual images in the pictures he displays?

3. Are the pictures warm and inviting rather than cold and impersonal?

4. Is there an element of the comical or whimsical?

5. Do you find his art collection appealing?

6. Are the images tranquil rather than violent or threatening?

7. Are the facial and bodily features attractive rather than distorted or ugly?

8. Is there an eclectic balance of pictures rather than a collection representing only one style?

9. Do the works reflect dreams as opposed to nightmares?

10. Do his pictures tend to be bright and colorful rather than dark and foreboding?

The Score

Tally up your score with the following points: All = 4 points; Many = 3 points; Some = 2 points; Few = 1 point; None = 0 points.

[31–40 points]

A warm, positive person with a bright and optimistic attitude toward life has selected this art. Fundamentally life-affirming, you can expect him to be loving and generous in a relationship. No emotional storms cloud his mind; no dark, lingering anger is likely to explode at any moment. Here is that rare individual who appreciates the beauty life has to offer and finds much to praise—and little to criticize—in the woman he loves.

[21–30 points]

Basically a positive and caring individual, this man has a few unresolved emotional dilemmas that add a dimension of tantalizing complexity many women find attractive. He often deliberately uses his art to make a social or political statement, and if you agree with his outlook, he is a good bet as a romantic partner.

[11–20 points]

There are multifaceted dimensions to this complex personality. His artwork reveals a personality schism in which he is sometimes bright, cheerful, and optimistic, and other times depressed and negative. There is some unresolved anger boiling inside this man, and if you become involved, you may find him to be a moody mystery. One day he'll surprise you with flowers, the next week say something cruel and uncaring. It is a challenge to learn how to respond to this well-meaning, but rather conflicted, guy.

[0–10 points]

By almost any measure, this individual is alienated and distant from emotional interaction. Inclined to see only the worst in people, he is highly suspicious and reclusive by nature. There will be far more pain and misery than compassion in this relationship and it is best to stay clear.

Different Strokes for Different Folks

Here's a brief analysis of some specific painting styles and an explanation of the Love Codes they project:

Abstract

As enigmatic to their owners as they are to viewers, abstract paintings deliberately lend an air of mystery to a home. A man who displays such imagery is one who believes that people are entitled to interpret reality in any way they see fit. Although he may be intrigued by life's unanswered questions, he's not concerned with arriving at firm answers. On the plus side, a man

attached to abstract art rarely approaches a relationship with hard-and-fast rules of appropriate behavior. But don't expect this guy to provide a clear definition of where you stand; after all, shrouding his true feelings is part of the fun.

Old Masters

Reproductions, one assumes, but nonetheless when you spot a Da Vinci or a Rembrandt hanging on the wall, you've found a man with some old-fashioned values. Conservative in lifestyle, but passionate about genius, this is a man who believes the finer things in life must withstand the test of time. There is an elegance to everything he does and despite his reserve and controlling manner, you may appreciate his romantic style. If you pride yourself on being a woman who acts like a lady, be prepared to share candlelit dinners with this gentleman.

Impressionism

Beneath those light-dabbled bursts of color and pointillistic landscapes are layers of meaning waiting to be unwrapped. The man who displays impressionist art tends to be analytical, a shrewd observer who probes beneath appearances and discovers depths hidden to the casual onlooker. Because he will scrutinize every detail in order to see to the core of an issue, this man is a shrewd judge of human nature. In a relationship he is likely to be a good listener and a perceptive observer who is willing to wait for a woman to open up to him.

Realistic

Art is simply a way to state facts, according to the collector of realistic works, who likes his paintings to be clear, direct, and accessible. Translate those qualities into his dealings with people, and you've found a man who wants to know where people stand, what they want and who they want it from. If his literalism seems to lack a touch of imagination, at least he will present no unpleasant surprises, nor will his expectations of you be unrealistic!

Avant-Garde

A restless probing spirit, this man is constantly on the prowl for dramatic new experiences and adventures. Not content merely to read about the latest trends, he's part of what fuels their success. He's a risk-taker, always in pursuit of new styles—traditional values don't hold much importance to him—and he'll introduce you to worlds you never even knew existed. If the cutting edge excites you, too, you can help make this relationship a hot one.

Primitive

The collector of primitive art is drawn to adventure of a very different sort. A lover of rituals and symbolism, he will travel to exotic and far-flung places in search of local color and mystery. Driven by his own set of myths about noble savages and tribal harmony, he tends to romanticize now-Western ways. You may have to give up some creature comforts to follow this man, but if you don't have all the conventional expectations of the urban upwardly mobile, he could open your eyes to new worlds.

Giving Him a Screen Test

Movies, one of the most popular forms of culture today, are an important measure of compatibility. Whether you prefer the excitement of the big screen or the intimacy of the VCR, it won't be long before you discover whether or not you and your man enjoy the same types of flicks. Equally important, you'll soon learn how well the two of you can discuss and evaluate the movies you see together.

Today's films appeal to almost every taste imaginable, from the obscurely artistic to the mesmerizingly violent. Because each one makes a statement about values that prompts an emotional reaction from the viewer, you can learn a lot about a man's Love Codes from his film preferences.

LOUIS: THE FOREIGN FILM PEDANT

> JoAnna: Louis and I were introduced at a book party and he invited me to see a revival of a Bergman film. After we saw the film, he took great pains to explain the significance of each scene in detail, including an analysis of the movements made by the camera.

In the course of the next month we saw the latest Truffaut movie, a Japanese film that I didn't understand, and something political from South America. After he dragged me to a 3 ½-hour picture from Rumania I finally blew my stack and said the next film we saw *had* to be in English. He looked at me with sheer horror and proceeded to deliver a lecture about the superficiality of American movies.

Louis's approach to JoAnna was far more patronizing than enlightening. By deliberately dominating their post-film discussions, he made genuine dialogue impossible. A man who tries to dazzle others with his insights and intellect is only spotlighting his own lack of confidence.

Louis's insistence on selecting films that *he* wanted to see, regardless of JoAnna's preferences, is a patent display of selfishness and suggests that he may need total control over any situation, which is hardly grist for an egalitarian relationship. This is a man who will only satisfy a woman willing to acknowledge his superior intelligence, cultural sophistication, and elitist attitude.

What Are Your Man's Movie Preferences?

Foreign

Of course, not all foreign film enthusiasts are like Louis. A passion for foreign films also suggests erudition and a broad vision of the world. Don't be intimidated by a man's enthusiasm for foreign movies. If there is mutual respect in your relationship, you can learn from him without allowing him to dominate. Perhaps you can strike a pact, alternating between foreign and American films. If he respects your choices, he'll think that's a fair deal; if not, good riddance!

Famous Fatales

The worlds inhabited by Betty Grable, Joan Crawford, and Lauren Bacall have long past, but it is not hard to find the man who still honors their memory. They see classic films of the 1930s, 1940s, and 1950s over and over and often feel dissatisfied with contemporary mores—and the women the times have spawned. Some men who watch these films to the exclusion of other genres often feel like misfits. Although their manners may be refreshingly old-fashioned, they are often unrealistic about their relationships, approaching them through the distorted lens of a distant era.

Action/Adventure

A man enamored of such movies usually admires the strength and resourcefulness of their male stars. At bottom is usually a fear of his own impotence, which he will try to hide beneath a blustery, macho exterior. The occasional escape into the fantasy world of the action/adventure movie is a reasonable release, but an obsession with such films to the exclusion of all others reflects deep frustration. Such a man may be preoccupied with attempting to prove his "manhood" to you.

Documentary

Whether it is a film about racism in South Africa or the lives of Appalachian coal miners, the man who regularly attends documentaries is usually serious, socially conscious, and concerned about the welfare of others. Films are no means of release to this guy; rather, they are a tool that enables him to learn more about the world around him. If you share his sensibilities and concerns, there's a good bet here, but don't expect too much frippery from this guy. He takes life seriously and is looking for a woman who does, too. He makes firm commitments and sees them through.

Westerns

The plot of most Westerns is built around a simplistic portrayal of good against evil. Because the moral questions raised are answered clearly and without ambivalence, these films appeal to solid, unpretentious men. You'll find the Western enthusiast to be practical and to have both feet solidly on the ground, but don't expect him to cope with the complex issues that most contemporary films tackle. Such a man is strong-willed and a bit traditional in his outlook, but he knows the rules of proper behavior in a relationship and he'll fight for the woman he loves.

Horror

The need to test one's strength and courage is quite apparent in the man who feels compelled to see one horror film after another. He has a rather adolescent attitude, and you'll find that he has a hard time relaxing with you, because he feels obligated to prove he's not scared of you, a relationship, or anything.

Another type of man, though fewer in number, identifies with the victim. He feels terrible things have been done to him by life. For this reason, he's masking a great deal of anger and, in relationships, he may view himself the innocent victim of evil intent. See if he describes the women in his past as being monsters.

Comedy

The lover of comedy films is fortunate in possessing a good sense of humor, which can be vital to the survival of any involvement. He generally enjoys life and is optimistic, but it may be hard for him to discuss serious emotions. Although his feelings run deep, he sometimes conceals them by infusing his conversations with one-liners and humorous asides. You have to be able to deflect these in order to discover the sweet and sensitive person underneath.

Science Fiction

This man is an idealist with a utopian vision of the future. If you become involved with him, you'll open yourself up to a person who likes to try new things and is particularly fascinated by the latest technical gadgets. Never dismiss this man's favorite films as fantasy—true, he may cope with the problems of the present by escaping into the future, but he is also sensitive and profoundly concerned with building a better tomorrow.

We have seen how cultural preferences provide an important glimpse at a man's emotional makeup. Because he has an almost infinite collection of music, artwork, books, and films to choose from, his selections are a clear expression of his personality and his inclinations in a relationship. Be particularly certain to scrutinize any conflicts between his tastes—for example, the man who likes both Old Master paintings and rock-and-roll music is a complex individual who can not be readily pigeonholed, but may well be worth a closer look.

CHAPTER · **TWO**

HOW HIS LABOR WORKS IN YOUR UNION

There is a clear but complex connection between the way a man treats his professional colleagues and his friends and the way in which he will treat you. Although he often responds to a lover with a gentleness that he does not exhibit at work, it is rare for a man to undergo a complete transformation between his public and his private life.

There are exceptions, of course. A man who is known to be very aggressive and critical with his employees is said to be a real pussycat with his domineering wife; a man who is docile and acquiescent with friends may be more confident in asserting himself at home with his wife and children. Don't count on it though, and don't delude yourself by creating dreams based on false hopes. If a man is capable of a particular emotional reaction—whether it is anger, love, jealousy—with even one person, the proper stimulus can evoke the same reaction again. The greatest mistake a woman can make it is to believe that she can change a man's basic personality.

A Labor of Love

Research has shown that people choose their jobs to meet a range of psychological, intellectual, and creative needs. Men who are most satisfied with their work are in positions appropriate to their personality makeup. These are the men with a positive and self-confident outlook on life and they tend to be tolerant toward others and a pleasure to be with.

Men who are dissatisfied with their lot in life are often jealous and resentful of anyone who is happy, and they seek scapegoats for their disappointments. Such men will resent your optimistic perspective and make your life uncomfortable.

The answers to the following questions will help you identify the category into which your man falls.

Is His Job Working for Him?

Answer the following questions with: Always, Frequently, Occasionally, Seldom, or Never.

1. Does he blame others for his failures at work?

2. Does he value his own achievements regardless of the recognition he receives?

3. Is he more likely to criticize, rather than praise, the performance of his colleagues?

4. Is he cooperative, instead of suspicious, when management suggests a change in routine?

5. Does he feel jealous in the presence of other men, believing that they are more successful than he?

6. Does he seek to acquire the knowledge and expertise that will advance his career?

7. Is he content to relate only to people in his field, rather than expand his horizons?

8. Does he meet all his work deadlines?

9. Does he make work commitments that he can't fulfill?

10. Does he view criticism as a valuable tool that can help improve his job performance, rather than as a personal attack?

11. Does he seek new acquaintances primarily on the basis of what they can do for him?

12. Does he have a clear-cut agenda for achieving success through a series of well-planned steps?

13. Does he spend a lot of time lamenting lost opportunities and mistakes?

14. Does he appear to enjoy his job and speak about it with enthusiasm?

15. Is he highly competitive, determined to win at any cost?

16. Is he capable of striking a balance between work and his personal life?

17. Does he feel that he is in a rut, discouraged by his prospects but unable to do anything about them?

18. Does he tend to socialize with his co-workers?

19. Is he constantly annoyed or irritated by situations at work?

20. Does he believe that his job enables him to make the most of his creative and personal potential?

The Score

For questions with *even* numbers, score as follows: Always = 4 points; Frequently = 3 points; Occasionally = 2 points; Seldom = 1 point; Never = 0 points.

For questions with *odd* numbers, score as follows: Always = 0 points; Frequently = 1 point; Occasionally = 2 points; Seldom = 3 points; Never = 4 points.

[61–80 points]

Even more than having a positive outlook on his career, this man has the self-assurance and selflessness that signal a secure and motivated personality. He works well with others and is as eager to find a compatible relationship as he is to perform well on the job. And when he does find it, he will use his strength and resourcefulness to make it work.

[41–60 points]

This man is basically satisfied with his career, but he also harbors a certain degree of restlessness. From time to time he thinks that somewhere, perhaps, life has a little more to offer him. If he is able to express his reservations constructively, he is a good bet for an emotional involvement because he's aware of both the positive and negative aspects of his situation. Expect him to be able to make a solid emotional commitment.

[21–40 points]

This guy has some definite reservations about the direction in which his life is moving. Dissatisfied with a career that provides more frustrations than rewards, he tends to view his job as a way to survive rather than a source of fulfillment. Because he does not experience much pleasure from his work, he may expect a relationship to satisfy all his emotional needs. Beware a tendency to be demanding and critical.

[0–20 points]

Almost totally alienated from his job, this guy is angry and hostile, yet feels powerless to make real changes. A man caught in the grip of forces he cannot control, and indeed feels resentful of, makes a very poor choice as a potential mate.

What Is His Role in the Work Scene?

One man prefers a job without heavy responsibilities so that he can leave it behind when the day is over. Another wants to devote himself to his career with passionate commitment. Some men work alone, others thrive only in groups; some seek recognition in high-visibility fields, others work only for personal satisfaction.

Here are the Love Codes behind the way in which a man earns his daily bread and relates to the co-workers around him.

Boss Man

Most people who run their own businesses owe their success to hard work, shrewd politicking, and sheer talent. A man in charge may be a bit arrogant, believing himself smarter than anyone around him and resentful about ceding control. Independent, strong-willed, and stubborn, he is equipped to handle responsibility and knows how to behave in a position of authority.

It can be very difficult for the boss to take off that authoritative hat when he leaves the office, a trait that has its pros and cons in a relationship. This man is a good problem solver who accepts the necessity for hard work and he is a steady source of support in a crisis. The boss is used to giving orders, however, in the home as well as at work, and he expects his opinions to be respected. Many bosses are drawn to passive women, which is why women who abhor decision making may find the "bossy" man a godsend. More assertive women may find a relationship with this man a constant struggle.

Just a Job

The rank-and-file employee stands in marked contrast to the boss. He detests being in charge, does not want to take responsibility for others, and prefers the security of a structured role and a regular paycheck. This is the perfect man for a woman who likes to take over. He is happy to bring home his paycheck and let her pay the bills, make social arrangements, and generally organize their lives.

A man who is content to be a rank-and-file employee has chosen a relaxed and modest lifestyle over the rat race. If you are attracted to him because he's a laid-back, dependable family man, don't be surprised to discover that he's not terribly ambitious either on the job or in the home. As always, it is important to be realistic about what you really want.

Room at the Top

A man who has risen to the top ranks of a large corporation has learned to be a team player, to share responsibility, and to adapt to the needs of others—when they fit into his game plan. He is goal-oriented, ambitious, and focused on tangible achievements. There is not much room for spontaneity in this man's life and he doesn't welcome unexpected change, but his consistent, predictable, and straightforward approach makes many women feel secure.

Remember, though, that a top manager tends to take close personal ties for granted. Like the secretarial support staff he relies so heavily on, he sees close friends and family as indispensable, but often forgets to give them the tender, loving care they require. From time to time, you will have to shake his complacency and remind him of your importance in his life. Try mysteriously absenting yourself for one day a week and see how he feels about *that.*

On His Own

Although there is no one to tell him when to come to work or how to do his job, the man who works for himself, whether as a freelance writer or as a commission salesman, has a great deal of discipline and a strong sense of responsibility. He values independence more than security and is accustomed to being his own man, answering neither to bosses nor to employees.

A relationship with a self-employed man can be exciting, spontaneous, and unpredictable. He genuinely believes in egalitarian partnerships and will give you as much freedom as he demands back. Although this man doesn't make commitments readily, he sticks to the ones he chooses. He's an ideal partner for the woman who desires independence and assumes responsibility for herself. If you need a strong sense of stability, though, better look elsewhere.

Board Certified

Whether he is a lawyer, a doctor, or an architect, the professional man is often hotly pursued by women because he combines some of the best qualities of each of the men described previously. He has the confidence and independence to be a boss and the ability of a rank-and-file employee to acquiesce to ethical and legal codes of conduct.

Alas, the professional man tends to be somewhat impressed by his own importance. Because society endows him with high status and respects his authority, he often develops an attitude of superiority to others. You may have to struggle to penetrate his thick skin and uncover the vulnerability below. A man who thinks that he is a great catch for a lucky woman is often too arrogant to accept criticism or acknowledge any need to change. But if you're satisfied with him just the way he is, then you may indeed have a great catch!

Unemployed: Down or Out?

Many people are unemployed at some stage in their life for very legitimate reasons, and you'll need to know more about your man's history before making any generalizations based on his job status. Perhaps he is pursuing a creative or entrepreneurial career that has not yet gotten off the ground. He could be independently wealthy or chronically lazy, determined to find an appropriate outlet for his talents or unrealistic about his options for the future.

Being unemployed does not have to mean being unproductive and you can learn a lot about your man by asking these questions about his attitude:

- Does he have a positive outlook or is he morose and negative?
- Does he blame others for his predicament?
- Is he open to new and unexpected opportunities?
- Is he pursuing occupational leads?
- How does he spend his free time?

Although no one has a guarantee of finding an ideal job, a man who remains hopeful, patient, and positive is far more likely to come out on top of any situation. Someone who is depressed handicaps himself and turns off those around him. Your reactions during this period in his life will reveal as much about your ability to handle adversity as about his. They will also help to gauge the extent of your respect and devotion to this man.

The jobs described here, and many others, require a unique set of skills and reveal a great deal about your man's personality and his interest in a relationship. Some jobs, such as sales, are mostly people-oriented, and salesmen know how to put others at ease, which can be a real plus in a relationship. Or a job may force a man to deal with many underlings—the way he treats them reveals a lot about his respect for others, including you. By learning as much as you can about the type of work he does and how he does it, you will understand yet another important dimension of his personality.

CHAPTER · THREE

KNOW HIM BY THE COMPANY HE KEEPS

Most of us try to make a good impression when we meet someone new, especially in the early stages of courting. But we'll let down our guard with friends, especially people we know well. Matching a man's interactions with those who know him best and listening to what others say about him are thus likely to be very revealing. Forge ahead if they describe him as a loyal friend and a decent human being. Use caution if they jokingly call him a real pain but say they love him anyway—try to find out if there is more joke or more truth in their banter.

Analyze the anecdotes they tell about him. Is he the guy who saved the day by rounding up oversized tents when it rained for the family picnic? Or was he the one thrown out of a posh restaurant when he became drunk and disorderly? Is he thought of as someone who can be counted on in a jam or as someone who creates those jams?

Will He Be a Friend to You?

The first of the following statements applies to men who are reliable, friendly, outgoing, and sincere. The statement in parentheses is the opposite extreme and applies to men who are withdrawn, antisocial, and insecure. On a scale of 5 to 0, where a score of 5 means the first statement is 100 percent applicable, rate where he falls between the polar opposites.

1. He has welcomed you into his social world. (The opposite: He fails to introduce you to anybody.)

2. He calls his friends often. (The opposite: His friends have to pursue him.)

3. His friends believe him to be a man who always comes through in a pinch. (The opposite: He never extends himself to help others.)

4. He has friends of both sexes. (The opposite: All his friends are of one sex.)

5. He genuinely enjoys listening to someone else relate a story. (The opposite: He always tries to top the stories he hears.)

6. His pleasure in the accomplishments of his friends is evident and sincere. (The opposite: He is jealous of the achievements of others.)

7. He is modest about his own success. (The opposite: He inflates the importance of his achievements.)

8. He looks forward to going to parties. (The opposite: He attends parties purely out of a sense of obligation.)

9. He is very good at remembering names and faces. (The opposite: He rarely remembers the names of those he has met on previous occasions.)

10. He is always prompt for appointments. (The opposite: He is always late.)

11. He goes out of his way to help family or friends in trouble. (The opposite: His family and friends have to beg him for assistance.)

12. He tries to see events from other people's perspective. (The opposite: He passes judgment on others without bothering to understand their point of view.)

13. He is genuinely close to a number of people. (The opposite: All his relationships are casual and transitory.)

14. Many of his friendships extend back at least four or five years. (The opposite: Most of his friendships are of recent vintage.)

15. He usually gives people the benefit of the doubt. (The opposite: He is quick to condemn others.)

16. He uses his friends as a sounding board when he experiences setbacks. (The opposite: He suffers his disappointments in silence.)

17. When plans change, he can make the transition with a minimum of effort. (The opposite: He fusses endlessly about disruptions in his plans.)

18. He periodically hosts dinner or cocktail parties. (The opposite: He is the eternal guest.)

19. He sends cards or gifts to friends to commemorate holidays, birthdays, and anniversaries. (The opposite: He never remembers the special occasions of those close to him.)

20. He tries to get together with friends regularly. (The opposite: He seems indifferent to seeing his friends.)

The Score

Total up the points and read what your score means below:

[81–100 points]

This guy is refreshingly loyal, empathetic, and sincere. He makes an effort to stay in touch with many people, extends himself for his friends, and takes care of those close to him in time of need. These are rare attributes indeed in self-centered and narcissistic times, and his strong sense of values makes him a fine relationship catch. He is secure enough to allow you to blossom.

[61–80 points]

This man is enthusiastic and positive about life and generous and gregarious in a love relationship. He values his friendships and you can expect him to be very attentive and concerned with your well-being. Despite the value he places on friendship and love, however, there are a number of other priorities in his life.

[41–60 points]

This person takes a rigidly egalitarian view toward relationships—he is willing to give just what he receives, no more and no less. Unless he is sure you will respond to his affections with equal enthusiasm, he is not likely to be overly demonstrative. Expect your involvement with this man to evolve slowly and cautiously.

[21–40 points]

This man is something of a loner and you will have to make a concerted effort to keep your relationship going. It is difficult for him to get close to others because of the hard-to-penetrate defensive shields that he has erected. Even the most determined woman won't be able to penetrate all his barriers or force him to respond with as much depth of feeling as she would like.

[0–20 points]

Stay away! This guy borders on being completely antisocial, making little or no effort to extend himself to others. Indeed he seems to be wrapped so tightly in his emotional shell that he is virtually unresponsive. This is a clear sign that he doesn't care for himself enough to think he is worthy of even the most rudimentary contacts with others.

How Well Does He Share?

One of the questions that always arises when a couple first gets involved is how to relate to each other's friends. Some couples adopt the other's buddies wholesale and plan all social activities as a unit. Others insist on maintaining some independent friendships outside their primary love relationship. There are no rules to follow on this issue, but the choice a man makes tells you how he will treat you in a relationship.

SHARE AND SHARE ALIKE

> Fay: Being with Rick opened up a whole new world to me. He was an actor who knew all kinds of show-business people I would never have the opportunity to meet as a teacher in elementary school. I learned a lot from them and it also helped me understand Rick better.

A man who wants to share his friends demonstrates a generosity of spirit and a genuine respect for you. Proud of the friendships he has developed over the years and excited about your fledgling relationship, he is open enough to invite you to share an important part of his life. Rick clearly understands the importance of close connections, whether they are good friends or significant lovers.

Similarly, a man who really cares for you will want to get to know your friends better. We *should* judge each other by the company we keep, and a man will understand you better if he shares that part of your life, at least some of the time.

NEVER THE TWAIN SHALL MEET

> Sheila: Simon socialized with a lot of people, but he never invited me to go out with them. He divided his weekend so

that we would spend one night together and he would go out alone with his friends on the other night. Although we had been dating for six months, I had never even met his best friend. I really resented being kept in one small compartment of his life.

Although a man is certainly entitled to spend time alone with his friends, Simon's refusal to introduce Sheila to important people in his life suggests that he is not totally committed to their relationship, and therefore does not want to mingle it with the more permanent elements in his life. His reluctance to share his friends indicates a selfish streak, as well. Be prepared to bicker about sharing expenses and household chores, too.

In a similar vein, some men resent the time or emotional energy that a woman devotes to anyone besides him. By couching his resentment toward your friends in terms that emphasize his love for you ("But, Dana, don't you *want* to spend as much time together as we can?"), a man can be deliberately manipulative. Don't be fooled, though—true love is expansive, not restricting, and his resentment is no sign of love.

NOT A FRIEND IN THE WORLD

Jody: It really bothered me that Isaac had no friends of his own and no interest in my friends either. I had so many friends, and I thought there was something wrong with him. I hated leaving the house and seeing him sit on the couch so forlorn—like a lost puppy dog. And he certainly did his best to make me feel guilty about leaving him alone. That was the worst part of it—he was so dependent on me because he had no one else to turn to.

A man's lack of male friends is a source of irritation and unhappiness to many women. Women are often initially attracted to a man who is emotionally dependent because he is reassuring and attentive early in their meetings—often when she feels uncertain and eager for commitment. Only later, when she feels more secure and ready to resume her "normal" pattern, will she recognize that this loving and responsive puppy dog is really an albatross.

Be warned that a man without friends usually finds it very difficult to be close to others and does not readily share his feel-

ings. Although he will rely on you to satisfy his emotional needs, it may be difficult to drag him from the shell in which he has encased his emotional self.

YOUR FRIENDS ARE HIS FRIENDS

> Rhonda: It was a good thing that Gary didn't have any friends of his own, because I am so involved with mine that I insist on spending a lot of time with them. It has worked out perfectly because he is willing to adopt all my friends as his own.

For emotional and cultural reasons, many men simply do not have friends with whom they can share confidences. Others feel they have to cut ties with their past when they become involved with a woman. But when a man is without friends because of circumstance, rather than because he is emotionally withdrawn, he will happily embrace your friends. In the process he makes a significant statement about your importance in his life. Kudos for the man who accepts and respects you and seeks intimate bonding by sharing your life.

Keeping Your Friends to Yourself

Not all women are grateful for a man who is eager to share her friends. Perhaps you are reluctant to make that final commitment to your lover or do not respect him quite enough to go public with him. Or, you may feel a bit insecure about your relationship and prefer to be the focus of *all* his attentions. Better take a close look at your own motives.

A man's own friendships—and his response to yours—can give you strong hints about his ability to sustain relationships, the kinds of emotional connections he values and, ultimately, about your compatibility. Keep in mind, though, that men and women often have different attitudes about the role of friendship in their lives. Male friendships traditionally focus more on shared activities and interests and less on shared feelings and personal revelations. As long as they do not become an excuse to avoid emotional exploration, those types of bonds can be just as meaningful.

CHAPTER · **FOUR**

GETTING THE PARTY
LINE ON HIM

Throughout this book we have discussed many personality traits that can clearly be categorized as either desirable or undesirable—selfishness, generosity, hostility, and affection, for example. But there are also many forms of social behavior that are neither good nor bad, only inappropriate for some people. In these cases, a man's desirability as a partner depends on *your* personality and needs.

One Woman's Meat . . .

In the case studies that follow, the differing reactions of two women to the same man show that the guy who is one woman's meat can be a poison for another.

JACK: THE LIFE OF THE PARTY

> Yvette: Jack is a friendly and gregarious man and he is known as the life of the party. He makes everyone feel at ease, but the truth is that I never enjoy being with him in a big crowd. As

soon as we get to a party, he immediately takes over and totally obscures me. He'll tell these god-awful salesman jokes filled with sexual innuendos. I am sometimes embarrassed to be with him.

Julia: I really thrive on going to parties with Jack. People flock to him because he is funny and enthusiastic and open. He blazes the trail for us to meet everyone at the party. I'm a little shy and it certainly is convenient to have such a ready entrée in a crowd of strangers.

A man who is the life of the party thrives on being the center of attention and is often a genuine crowd-pleaser. The need to dominate a group, however, can also indicate a person who is far from confident about himself. By the same token, his sexually-laden humor could signal a level of discomfort with the real thing—or it could mean that he's a man to whom sex is particularly important.

Yvette is dismayed and put off by Jack's behavior and resents playing second fiddle to him. She needs to find the man who is more reserved and willing to let her share the limelight. Julia, on the other hand, profits from all the attention Jack receives. Not one who seeks attention herself, she thrives in his reflected glory.

JOSE: THE MAN'S MAN

Monica: When I go to Jose's house it is like attending an ongoing bachelor party. He'll invite the guys over to watch football and baseball games and, like most men, they seldom clean up after themselves. When they aren't watching sports together, they all go off on hunting and fishing excursions, leaving me feeling lonesome and irritated. Jose is always very affectionate, but I am unhappy that we have so little time alone together.

Sally: There was a time when I thought that Jose must be gay because he seemed to want to spend all his time with his male friends. He works with men, spends his evenings with men, takes vacations with men. He never even talks to women at parties—instead I'll spot him in a corner sharing a laugh with the usual gang of guys.

I really value my independence and need space and time to pursue my own interests, so my relationship with Jose has been perfect. I don't have to worry that he is with another woman and, when we are together, he is very affectionate. We genuinely enjoy each other's company but we spend a lot of time apart.

Men like Jose are accustomed to the company of men and share a camaraderie with them that they simply cannot replicate with women. Although Jose is genuinely affectionate and appreciates loyalty, his social needs are largely satisfied by his colleagues at work and his buddies at home. When he does crave the warmth that only a woman can provide, he is grateful—if you will accept him on his terms.

Monica, who is looking for a relationship in which she can spend most of her spare time with the man she loves, feels anger and frustration with Jose. Sally, however, finds exactly what she needs from him. Many independent women find it highly advantageous to be involved with a "man's man" because they have the security of commitment without the pressure of confinement.

ROGER: FLIRTATIOUS BUT NOT FICKLE

Rita: I know that Roger is a big flirt, but frankly I thrive on the fact that he's attractive to every woman who meets him. It's an ego trip, I admit, but I get a kick from the envy of other women. When a woman is really coming on strong to him, I get a pang of insecurity but I realize that Roger flirts because he needs to be reassured about his desirability.

Judy: I stopped seeing Roger after just a few dates because of his flirtatious behavior. He kept assuring me that he was genuinely interested in pursuing a relationship, but he also wanted every woman in the room to pay attention to him. After a while, I decided I wanted someone who considered me woman enough.

It takes a very confident woman to be comfortable with a ladies' man, but Rita is right—Roger's compulsive flirtation is a compensation for his feelings of inadequacy, not a search for another woman. A man who is genuinely fond of women tends to have a lot of close female friends and he can be a warm and communicative partner to someone special. If you're at peace with the green-eyed monster of jealousy, all signals are go here.

Insecure women need to beware, however. Watching her man flirt in a crowd sent shivers through Judy, and she could never relax when she was out with Roger or he was out alone. Although he frequently reassured her of the depth of his feelings, he never stopped flirting because he needed continual reassurance. Second thoughts are in order for a woman who seeks a man's undivided attention.

SEAN: NO FLASH BUT A LOT OF SUBSTANCE

Maxine: Sean is a terrific guy but I certainly didn't realize it when friends introduced us at a party. He was cordial but seemed terribly ill at ease. I would never have gone out with him except that our mutual friends kept telling me what a great guy he was. When we finally got together for dinner, I was amazed at how relaxed and interesting he turned out to be.

> Iris: Sean certainly commands a lot of respect among the people who know him best, but I can't help thinking he's a little dull. I was reluctant to go out with him the first time, and my friends practically had to twist my arm to convince me to give him a second chance. I'm sure he's a genuinely decent person but I like a man with some fire, someone that other people notice. A shrinking violet just isn't my speed.

Men who seem quiet may actually be very shy, able to emerge from their shells only in social settings in which they feel comfortable and accepted. Some men are particularly shy with women but very much at ease with male friends or colleagues; others are able to relax with outgoing women who can initiate the conversation and do not have hard-and-fast definitions of proper social skills.

Women often fail to measure the true depths of bashful men who may offer more substance and commitment than a more glamorous personality. In a relaxed one-on-one situation, Maxine was pleasantly surprised by Sean's attributes. Iris, however, knew that she wanted a man with a lot more dazzle and spark than Sean. She was right to stop seeing him. After all, there is no point in continuing an unsatisfying relationship. Many unhappy marriages are the result of such inertia.

CLARK: MR. PRIVATE

> Kitty: Clark is always so mysterious and reserved about what he does and who he does it with that it adds to the excitement of our being together. Our relationship is built on the basis of mutual respect for each other's privacy. I really appreciate the

space he gives me, and I try to give him the same. I've always been uncomfortable about having to account for my whereabouts.

Melody: Clark's insistence on his privacy leaves me feeling intrusive if I ask even the most casual question, such as where he had lunch. I like a little breathing room myself, but this man doesn't know the meaning of intimacy. He never shares his feelings with me and I know very little about the people or activities that keep him occupied. When we get together we are like two people who have no existence outside of each other!

People who rigorously guard their privacy tend to be vulnerable and suspicious of the motives of others. Unconsciously, they feel that any information they volunteer can be used against them. A man who is cautious about revealing himself to a woman shows his lack of trust in her.

By deliberately shrouding himself in an enigmatic mystique, Clark is able to choose the image that he wishes to project; in doing so, he maintains power over the women in his life. To Kitty, the sense of mystery fuels excitement about the relationship, conveying the notion that Clark is a man of many levels. Melody, however, resents the way in which he sets up a barrier that impedes their closeness.

Remember that it is impossible to develop an intimate relationship with an intensely private person unless he loosens up. Drawing him out will grow tiresome, as will his accusations that you are invading his private space. Even Kitty is likely to grow more irritated and less intrigued by Clark's mysterious facade.

Masking His Identity: Public versus Private Persona

The face that we show to our professional associates and casual acquaintances may sometimes differ from the face that we show our close friends and lovers. However, if the image a man projects publicly is so radically different from the man you know privately that you have to make a major adjustment when you change environments, you may feel that you are leading a schizophrenic existence.

THE LION THAT'S REALLY A PUSSYCAT

> Roxanne: Brad is so sweet when we're alone together at home—he is really a liberated man. We divide all the household tasks equitably, and he always makes it very clear how much he values our relationship. But when we are out of the house he is entirely different. He becomes very aggressive and macho, insisting on conducting all the communications with waiters and taxi drivers, for example. And he joins in when other men put down their wives and talk about how difficult women are.

This guy may be a sweetheart but he doesn't want the world to know it. On one level, he has accepted the premises of liberation and makes a genuine effort to do his fair share. On another level, however, he maintains some old-fashioned, macho ideas about how a "real man" should behave. Brad clearly has some conflicts about an egalitarian relationship; by dominating Roxanne in public and complaining to others about her, he is trying to lay to rest any notion that he is wimpy or henpecked.

Approach with caution. These vestiges of his upbringing will not be easily dispatched. You can try, however, by making him aware of what he is doing and how it makes you feel. When you are together in a group, go a little overboard to give him center stage. Let him hear you boasting to others about how strong and successful he is. Although his egalitarian approach to household chores is admirable, find other attributes besides his dishwashing and housekeeping abilities to praise in public.

DR. JEKYLL AND MR. HYDE

> Sylvia: My life with Greg would be wonderful if we spent all our time together with other people. In public he is kind, generous, thoughtful, and affectionate. More than one friend of mine has told me that I am the luckiest woman in the world. But it is all some sort of perverse act. As soon as we walk through the doors of the house, an instant transformation takes place. He becomes critical, nasty, angry, and selfish, and I can do nothing right.

Greg's public image represents only one side of his multifaceted and generally confused personality. Why is his private persona so different? There are several possibilities, each with complex psychological roots. Being close to a woman intimidates some men because they fear the loss of their own identity in a relationship. Some men resent their own dependencies and needs and in a perverse way turn this resentment against the woman to whom they are close. Other men have unrealistic expectations of a relationship and blame the woman for cheating them of their fantasy.

Whether the disparity between his public and private persons has roots in this man's family history or in his emotional past, it will not be easy to dissipate his private anger. He is definitely a candidate for therapy—but will almost surely react with hostility when you suggest it. Without change, you will never be happy with this man.

Early in your dating relationship, try to arrange social activities that give you the opportunity to watch your man work a crowd and relate to you in public. Certain facets of a man's personality come to life only in this environment, and it is best to get a glimpse of them before you get too deeply involved.

CHAPTER · **FIVE**

IS HE TUNED TO
YOUR SEXUAL
FRECUENCY?

There is probably nothing so steeped in legend, lore, and fantasy as sex. It is the arena in which contented couples remind each other of the depths of their love and the theater where the discontented express their frustration and anger. The bedroom is an adult playground where, in the best of times, the deepest intimacy possible between two human beings can be obtained.

More than 50 percent of the American population report sexual problems or dissatisfaction with their sex life. And this despite the sexual revolution of the 1960s, when the virtues of free love were widely touted and inhibitions were supposed to be shed. Who are the dissatisfied majority? Did they live through the revolution without ever taking a gun from their holsters? Do they suffer from personal inadequacy? Have they failed to read enough about the techniques of good loving? Probably not.

More likely they are people who accepted many of the newly granted freedoms licensed in the newspapers and on TV. In those days, the rule was: If you are attracted to someone, you should naturally have sex. And if you were sexually compatible, the relationship could be considered meaningful. In those days, all powers of decision making were handed over to the genitals. Women were told to do it and to talk about it. To search for their G-spots and to strive for multiple orgasms. To experiment with different partners and different positions. And to love it all!

But, as with so many revolutions, romantic myths have inevitably given way to harsher realities. Good sex has not proven to be a matter of keeping score or of racking up new partners and exotic experiences. Instead, most of us have finally discovered that sex is satisfying only when it is an integral part of an emotionally rich relationship. This chapter is aimed at helping you learn what you need to know to find the man who has also learned that lesson.

A Matter of Biology

Many women confuse the intimacy of sex with emotional intimacy and assume that a physically expressive man is equally open about his feelings. Conversely, many men distinguish sex from emotional involvement, compartmentalizing their feelings in a way that totally mystifies women. The tenderness of a man's lovemaking may as easily stem from his own need for closeness as from genuine feelings for a woman.

Like it or not, biology plays a big part in a man's sex drive. A man with a high sex drive may consciously perfect his techniques in order to enhance his sex appeal—and his own ego as well. Curiously, many men who lead lives on the fringe of conventional society are great lovers. Daunted by the tasks of competing in life, they focus their energies on developing powerful sexual connections with women.

A man with a low sex drive, by contrast, may never have given sexual behavior much priority and therefore feels inexperienced or inadequate in a sexual interaction. Otherwise successful and confident professional men often have hang-ups that stem from a fear of sexual intimacy.

A man's sexual nature, of course, is expressed not only in the sexual act itself but in the ease with which he makes casual physical contact, the sensual pleasures he enjoys, and the types of women to whom he is attracted. As you analyze a man's sexual proclivities, watch for Love Codes that tell you whether he is aggressive or passive, nurturing or demanding, aloof or intimate, dominant or submissive, faithful or philandering, caring or cruel, stable or unstable, imaginative or boring, and involved or indifferent.

Flirtatiousness: A Sign of Cruising or Courting?

A man who flirts either verbally or nonverbally is sending you a flattering message and you have the right to be pleased. Whether it is a sign of true affection, sexual attraction, or merely a passing compliment, however, depends on what follows next. Even if flirtation doesn't actually lead to sexual involvement, a man's approach reveals a lot about his attitudes and how he will conduct himself in a relationship.

Suggestive Signs

• **The Look in His Eye:** The suggestive way in which a man eyes you tells you a lot about his intent. A furtive glance, for example, suggests that he is interested, but finds you a bit intimidating. A raised eyebrow is a cockier sign, and a direct stare is a deliberate effort to pierce your defenses and sweep you off your feet.

• **Smilin' Through:** Another clue to the intention of his flirtatiousness is the sincerity of his smile. A warm, open smile suggests genuine interest; a tense or closed smile is a sign that the flirt is rather unsure of himself and may distrust women.

• **Whistling:** Although this is not the mark of a sophisticated man, whistling is generally harmless and is not intended as a serious flirtation. Men will usually whistle at a woman only when they are in the company of other men. It is a way of simultaneously acknowledging your appeal and declaring themselves off-limits at the same time.

• **Licking His Lips:** Although many women find this explicitly sexual gesture to be obnoxious and degrading, it is an indication of a sexually passionate man. If you are looking for thrills—and don't need much intellectual intercourse—he may be your man.

• **Humor:** A man with a sense of humor is charming and endearing enough to dispel potentially awkward situations with a clever remark. However, he is uncomfortable in the role of aggressor and needs you to give him the confidence to continue his advances.

• **Touching:** A man who touches you when you are first introduced is bold, confident, and sensual. He is ruled by his passions and uses that passionate nature as a means of asserting control in a relationship. If you share his sensual side, all signals are go here.

• **Complimenting:** Some men are sincere with their compliments, whereas others use flattery solely for the purpose of getting ahead. Pay attention to what he says—if he goes overboard in praising your beauty or intelligence, it is wise to be somewhat skeptical. But if his remarks are appropriate to the conversation, you may have found a man who is not afraid to say what he really feels.

Foreplay: A Taste of Things to Come

Most sexual encounters begin with arousing words, games, or other techniques to ease a couple from a social evening into a night of lovemaking. What a man likes to do prior to the main event hints not only at his abilities as a lover but at many other aspects of his personality. Along with analyzing his preferred methods of foreplay, watch his actions for these clues: Does he always initiate foreplay? Does he always like to do the same things before lovemaking? Does he linger to enjoy foreplay or does he rush through it?

Massage

It is hard to go wrong with a man who wants to trade massages. He communicates patience and caring as he strokes and kneads those knots from your body. Here is a man who understands the sources of tension in the modern world and responds to a call for help in times of trouble. High praise for someone who knows that a good massage is a fine way to begin a relaxing evening of lovemaking.

Necking and Petting

A wise and thorough man knows slow and arousing stimulation starts from the top down. Necking is the traditional method of working into sex, and for good reason; it is a way of gradually building intimacy and excitement. The man who enjoys necking and petting has a strong sentimental side to him and is capable of great infatuation.

Sexual Films and Photos

Although looking at sexual films and photos can be a stimulating and interesting diversion for a couple, men usually find them much more arousing than women. Be careful here—the man who always looks at visual erotica prior to sex is not adequately attracted to his own partner. He is keeping women at a distance in order to avoid feeling vulnerable to them.

Dressing Up

A man who wants to dress in costume before he undresses for lovemaking has a unique and playful imagination. His lack of inhibitions and refreshingly unself-conscious nature translate nicely into creative lovemaking. Be cautious about his intentions, though. If he always insists on dressing up, watch out! This man doesn't really want to be with *you*.

Sharing Fantasies

Fantasies are a good way to warm up to serious sexual activity. Even very close couples are sometimes too inhibited to share their deepest, darkest secrets, and a man who is willing to expose his fantasies to your scrutiny is able to open up in other realms of his life as well. Sharing fantasies is also a fine tool to improve intimate contact.

Buzzing on Booze or Pot

Some men use a little alcohol or marijuana to relax before a sexual encounter. In moderation, some drugs can intensify physical sensations and increase pleasure, but in excess, they are more likely to make him limp, not aroused. A man too ill at ease to enjoy sober sex probably has other emotional problems that will surface in the course of your relationship.

Bubble Bath

Taking a bubble bath together is a sensual way to begin an evening together. You both emerge relaxed, aroused, and reassured that anything can safely go in the bedroom. You can look hopefully at the man who suggests a warm bath before bed.

Portraits of Sexual Pursuers

The sexual magnetism that draws lovers together is powerful and mysterious. People are attracted to each other for many reasons, and it is not always possible to understand just why. One thing is certain, however: Women are drawn to men who can meet their emotional needs, whatever those may be. Whether it is for a single night or for a lifetime, a woman looks to a man for the comfort, security, passion, commitment, or pain she unconsciously craves.

In the following section, we provide sketches of some of the men who inhabit the sexual landscape and explain what their behavior means to a sexual relationship.

Don Juan

The perennial "ladies' man" charms, flatters, and seduces any woman he can—and makes her feel wonderful about it. A man said to be a Don Juan actively pursues a coterie of different ladies and is in no hurry to settle down with any of them.

> Dory: When I first spotted John at a party, my internal warning system told me that he was a flirtatious ladies' man. My rational side warned me to be cautious, but my passionate side took no heed. When John held me close and whispered those tender words of appreciation, I felt myself begin to soar. And when we made love, his caress was so tender I felt as if our souls were merging. By the next morning I was in love and ready to run off together into the sunset. And John was prepared to run off into the sunrise, appreciative of a lovely but final evening together.

Don Juans are men who live for the moment, and during that moment they are genuinely tender and appreciative. But they are inherently restless, fearing intimacy as much as they need it, often avoiding long-term attachments to mask a deep-seated dependency. At parties, you can recognize them because they are surrounded by attractive women, and they ask for every phone number in the crowd. Well-meaning friends are also certain to point them out as men who have left a string of old lovers behind.

Most Don Juans eventually settle down, but only when the desire to start a family or the feelings of loneliness become over-powering. And even then, sexual fidelity never becomes their strong point. They are constantly battling a sense of suffocation and may flirt or even have an affair simply to reaffirm their independence.

Sexual Skidoo

A man who plays the game of sexual skidoo may seem genu-inely interested in you, but he disappears from sight after the first time you sleep with him. What's going on here?

> Krista: If I am really interested in a man, I might want to spend the night with him. But even after things go really well, I have been with men who left the next morning and never called me again. It didn't seem to matter how long it took to have sex—whether I held out till the third date or the tenth date, after sex he disappeared. After all these years I still can't tell when a man is really interested in a relationship or just another sexual conquest.

Although the notion is an archaic one, there *are* still men who pursue women with the goal of sexual conquest. Try not to take rejection personally. A man who heads for the hills after having sex with a woman assumes she will make demands on his time and emotional energies. Perhaps he has had genuinely bad experiences with clinging women, but more likely he is simply afraid of intimacy.

Screening Out the Sexual Skidoo

Here are clues that suggest your man may not hang around for too long:

- He falls madly in love and hotly pursues you without knowing who you really are.
- He tells you everything you've always wanted to hear—that you're wonderful and that he's been looking for someone like you his whole life.
- He is too physically expressive, touching and stroking you before you are on intimate terms.
- He's never been involved in a long relationship.
- Rumor or his own information suggests that a lot of women have passed through his life.
- He is boastful or patently dishonest about his background.
- He shows off by spending a lot of money.
- He plies you with alcohol or drugs.
- He is overly eager to have sex *before* you go out together.

Snaring the Sexual Skidoo

Although sexual skidoo usually signals the fear of commitment, there are ways to overcome his mistrust. If you are interested in pursuing a relationship with this man, you will have to convince him that you are perfectly comfortable with casual, obligation-free dating.

Here is how to convey that message:

- Steer clear of talk about commitment and relationships. Even if you are speaking abstractly, this is sure to make him nervous.
- Let him know that you have an active social life. Date other men and chat casually about your social and professional pastimes. Don't say yes each time he asks you out.
- Don't always press him to arrange plans for your next rendezvous.
- Beat him to the punch by saying that although you like him and enjoy his company, you prefer to play the field for a while.
- Do not have sex on the first date.

If you reassure your man enough to begin dating on a regular basis, you will have to determine his desire for a permanent relationship by reading other Love Codes: Is he interested in you and your activites? Is he attentive and caring? Do you share the same goals and values? Does he have close male friends? What is his relationship history? Is he at a phase in life when commitment makes sense?

Once he finally decides to make a commitment, this man can be surprisingly faithful and dependable.

Passive Passion

The passive man is someone afraid to make the first move. He looks for aggressive women who will take charge.

> Monica: I knew Evan was really interested in me, but he was awkward and hesitant so I finally made the first pass. I was not surprised when he responded enthusiastically, but then he kept stepping away to ask me what I liked. I didn't want to discourage him, though, so I made some specific suggestions. He was agreeable to everything I wanted and amazingly had no problem performing!

Evan's ability to respond sexually was predicated on Monica's willingness to reassure and guide him. Although a passive man lacks the self-confidence to initiate sexual activity, he is generally able to open himself up both physically and emotionally once he knows what is expected of him. Evan's timidity will drive some women away, but with patience and a bit of imagination, others will find him a nurturing lover and a devoted partner. He is sensitive to your needs and accepts your ideas in guiding the relationship.

Caution: Do not confuse passivity with passive–aggressiveness. A passive–aggressive man harbors anger beneath his placid exterior and is more likely to lash out at you than to respond to your well-intended suggestions.

Aggressive Amour

> Mary: Gene was overtly sexual and up-front about his desires, and I was really turned on by the sexual self-confidence he exuded. I wasn't disappointed either. He was a master performer and a thorough, concerned lover. Although I'm not usually so passive, Gene seemed determined to take control, and I was willing to lie back and just indulge myself.

An aggressive lover can be very exciting to a woman, because surrendering control plays an important role in many sexual fantasies. Although the stereotype is a very traditional one, many women still seek a man who is powerful enough to sweep her off her feet.

A man who projects blunt sexuality and the promise of passionate lovemaking so unabashedly is very confident about his abilities in bed. The price of such confidence is often detachment, however. Men who are more emotionally involved in their sexuality are not always able to perform as instantaneously and with as much control. The psychic support you get from this guy is likely to be minimal.

Slow and Sensual

Paula: Max and I can kiss for hours before we even get around to stroking each other. Our physical rapport is slow and sensual as though each part of our body is communicating its own messages. Making love with Max is like having a seven-course banquet. I love the variety and the pacing. Every once in a while, though, I would enjoy skipping the gourmet dinner and just having a hot dog on the run.

A sensual man perceives each part of lovemaking as meaningful and special in its own right. Reaching orgasm is not his driving goal; rather, it is the process of getting there that provides him the most satisfaction. Even though you may never succeed in getting a sensual man to forego the fullness of each sexual experience, the consolation is that he cares enough about you to take time with you in other ways, too—sharing thoughts, listening to your concerns, and lending his support when you need it.

An impatient woman—or one who is not completely comfortable with sex—may become frustrated with the tempo, but if you can slow down to his speed, you are likely to discover new ways to appreciate familiar experiences.

Carnal Knowledge: The Position He Puts You In

Although the Karma Sutra lists more than 600 sexual positions, many couples quickly find a few favorites and then experiment with others over time. Variety is an important sexual spice, and in a healthy partnership a couple explores new positions not only to prevent staleness but for the thrill of shared adventure. Similarly, there are many ways to stimulate each other to orgasm, and secure lovers are not afraid of experimentation.

From the first time you and your partner make love, you should observe the sexual positions he prefers and the ways in which he attains—and helps you attain—orgasm.

1. Does he usually want to make love in the classic missionary position where he is on top and you are on the bottom?
2. Does he prefer positions in which you face away from him?
3. Does he experiment with new positions?
4. During lovemaking is he constantly changing positions faster than you would like?
5. Does he insist on controlling all sexual maneuvers?
6. Is he preoccupied with attaining mutual orgasm or otherwise focused on the orgasm rather than the total experience?
7. Can he reach orgasm only through oral sex?
8. Only through masturbation?
9. Does he attempt to delay orgasm (when he can) so that you can reach yours (when you're close)?

If he usually prefers face-to-face intercourse and experiments with a variety of sexual positions and styles of achieving orgasm, this man seeks intimacy and interacts comfortably with his sexual partners. On the contrary, if he prefers not to face his partner, focuses single-mindedly on achieving orgasm or usually masturbates to reach it, and shifts sexual positions frequently, he is avoiding intense emotions and close personal involvement. There is reason to doubt his ability or interest in making emotional commitments.

Responses that indicate rigid patterns—such as the man always being on top, or orgasm being achieved exclusively through oral sex—signal a need for control that undoubtedly extends beyond the boundaries of the bedroom. Proceed with extreme caution. This man neither understands, nor cares much about, practicing the art of a shared relationship. He views women primarily as objects to serve him.

Postcoital Pleasures and What They Measure

The way in which a man treats you after making love is as revealing as foreplay. This is a vulnerable period for you, and his behavior after sex is a window to his true feelings about you.

Hugs and Holds You

This man feels protective and loving and expresses those emotions not only during lovemaking but at many other times as well. Your emotional support means a great deal to him.

Wants to Talk

The Love Codes in this behavior depend on the topics he raises. It can be a time for frank conversation, when he speaks endearingly of your importance in his life and when you feel very close. But if talks about things that are totally irrelevant to the two of you, it could be a sign, once again, that he doesn't want you to get too close.

Eats

It can be fun to share a snack together—whether it is cold chicken or ice cream—after the exertion of lovemaking. This is a healthy sign that shows he is relaxed and comfortable with you—unless he really gorges himself. This suggests that he feels dissatisfied and has to fulfill himself in other ways.

Smokes a Cigarette

A leisurely smoke after lovemaking may seem like a fine way to relax, but it also puts some distance between you. As involved and passionate as he is during lovemaking, he also finds the experience anxiety producing and may have some problems with exposing his emotions.

Goes to the Bathroom

If he visits the bathroom only briefly, you can assume this is a normal physiological function. If he disappears for a long period of time, however, it indicates that he is trying to escape emotional responsibilities and probably feels uncomfortable with intense involvements.

Washes Up

Although cleanliness may be next to godliness, it is not a good sign after evening sex. It usually discloses discomfort with natural body functions and a feeling that sex itself is dirty.

Turns on the Television

If he snaps on the tube the instant you have finished making love, he may be avoiding you, and there is reason for concern. If he hugs and kisses you for a while, first, then watching TV with you at his side is only a tool for further relaxation.

Goes to Sleep

Nothing is more disconcerting to a woman than the man who immediately goes to sleep after climaxing, because it makes her feel that she is being used merely as a sexual object. If this becomes a regular pattern, this man doesn't really want to be intimate with you. He is expressing his anxiety and detachment with a snore.

Is He Really Your Dream Guy?

There are few better ways to gauge a person's true emotional state than the position in which he sleeps after you have made love.

MATTHEW: SPREAD-EAGLED AND DOMINANT

> Cara: Matthew has a spacious queen-size bed in his apartment, but after sleeping with him a few nights I realized that he didn't really like to share it with anyone. He sleeps spread-eagled across the entire bed as though he is the only one there. And he sleeps so deeply that a gentle nudge has no effect whatsoever.

Just as he dominates the bed, so Matthew must dominate every other situation in which he finds himself. Powerful and uncompromising, he insists on making all the decisions for people around him and demands to be the center of attention. It is not only space that he allocates parsimoniously—he gives grudgingly of his emotions as well. Be prepared for a relationship with a man who shares himself only on his terms.

Other Sleeping Positions

Fetal

Sleeping in the fetal position reflects the desire to return to the safety of the womb. The man who sleeps most securely curled up into a ball seeks a woman who can provide the maternal qualities he yearns for. He wants a woman of strength and resourcefulness who will nurture his talents and provide refuge for him at the end of the day.

Spoon

A man who wraps his body around you while he sleeps is unconsciously helping you feel protected and loved. He thrives on playing the role of provider, has a strongly romantic streak to his personality, and will do almost anything to make your life safe and secure. By contrast, if he wants you to spoon around him, he has strong dependency needs and will expect you to be protective and reassuring. If you alternate spooning each other, your relationship is likely to be a mutually satisfying and inter-dependent one.

Flat-Out

Lying on his back with his legs straight out and hands clasped on his stomach, this man is mature, realistic, and devoid of illusions about the world. If you aren't looking for a starry-eyed romantic, you will find him generous and sympathetic to your needs. He has the confidence to face a crisis head-on and to fight for his principles. In a relationship he is calm and rational; only the utmost emotional provocation can make him lose his cool.

Belly Down

Sleeping on his stomach displays confidence and a sense of security. He can literally turn his back on the world without feeling suspicious or anxious. If you become more deeply involved with him, no doubt this quality of self-assurance will become even more apparent. By sleeping on his stomach, however, he is also protecting his genitals. This indicates that, despite his passion, he likes to call the shots when he's ready to make love.

Fists Clenched

This is a combative position and it discloses unresolved anger that has accumulated either during the day or between the two of you. There's something troubling him and you have to be able to find out what it is. Sleeping with his fists under the pillow means he's the type who hides his anger, whereas exposed fists reveal that he's more open about expressing his feelings.

Arms and Legs Crossed

Legs crossed shows a particular reticence about engaging in sexual relations, because it is one more way of guarding the genitals. Arms crossed is a way of maintaining distance. In a very real sense, he's not allowing his heart to come close to yours. Before he'll let his guard down, a man who sleeps in this position has to be convinced of your genuine concern and affection for him.

On the Edge

The man who moves all the way over to the edge of the bed is usually a passive person who is anxious to please and fearful of confrontation. Despite his protestations that he is concerned only about your comfort, he is also avoiding the intimacy of cuddling together, a reticence likely to carry into other components of a close relationship.

Turning His Back

By burying his head in the pillow and turning his back to you, your man is detaching himself from all the upsets of the day, and from his personal relationships as well. Although this position demonstrates his confidence that he has everything under control, it also suggests a capacity to hide his true emotions that is often disturbing to the women he is with.

Performance Anxiety: What He Really Fears

It should come as no surprise that anxiety, the plague of contemporary times, readily intrudes into the bedroom. Not only are we literally naked during sex, but we are also stripped of our usual defenses. Verbal maneuvers and dossiers of achievement serve no purpose. There is no way to cover up our physical shortcomings and little hope of masking our insecurity. In short, we are forced to be ourselves in bed, an intimidating prospect that can heighten a man's sense of vulnerability.

Increased aggressiveness, distancing, rigidity, and emotional withdrawal are all expressions of tension—a major factor in inhibiting sexual performance. Because he is so emotional, an anxious man can be very caring and loyal if he is not defeated by his own anxiety. It may be a struggle, however, to dissuade him from looking for excuses for his own discomfort, such as "I wasn't really turned on."

Why Can't He Relax?

Here are some of the reasons a man becomes anxious in bed:

- He is self-conscious and uncomfortable about beginning a new relationship.
- Because he is overly eager to please, he focuses more on his performance than on the joy of mutual pleasure.
- He fears women and generally avoids close relationships.

- He has a history of unsatisfactory sexual experiences or suffers from feelings of inadequacy in many realms of his life.
- Physiology often has a role to play in performance anxiety; a man who is not in top physical form may feel uncomfortable or self-conscious about his own body.

How Can I Assuage His Anxiety?

- Don't blame yourself. A man who is anxious is not intentionally rejecting the woman he is with. The problem is often quite the opposite— too much desire, not too little.
- Regardless of the cause of his anxiety, your reassurance and acceptance can work wonders. If he knows that you are not judging him and that you can be sexually satisfied in many ways other than intercourse, a man may be able to overcome his fear as he becomes more comfortable with you. Don't be surprised, however, if he feels so embarrassed by his sexual performance that he simply vanishes from your sight.
- Watch for behavioral signs that suggest he is anxious about sex. These can include physical symptoms, such as cold hands, sweaty palms, or rapid breathing; a race through the preliminaries of foreplay, a reluctance to sit close to you, or obvious awkwardness in his mannerisms. If you want to save this budding relationship, try to slow down the progression into the bedroom, regardless of the pressure he exerts.

Does He Harbor Homosexual Tendencies?

A startling number of men have had homosexual encounters or fantasies in their life. Although a single experience certainly does not signal a closet homosexual, frequent experiences or fantasies over a long period of time suggest that latent homosexuality may be lodged deep in a man's psyche. Whether or not he ever acts on his feelings, or even becomes consciously aware of them, they can interfere with his ability to love a woman deeply. Latent homosexuality often lies at the root of a man's unwillingness to make a commitment.

Answer "Yes" or "No" to each of the following questions and tally the total number of "Yes" responses:

1. Does he rail against homosexuality to the point of obsession?

2. Has he had several adult homosexual experiences or does he fantasize about them?

3. On social occasions, is he very reserved and formal in expressing affection toward other men?

4. Or is he so affectionate with his male friends that you feel uncomfortable?

5. Has he told you that gay men periodically make passes at him?

6. Does he feel compassion toward his mother who he views as a victim of his father's rage?

7. Is he especially resentful of the way his mother seduced, rejected, or tried to control him?

8. Does he like to tease or make jokes at the expense of homosexuals?

9. Are there times when he suggests another man join the two of you for a sexual "threesome"?

10. Does he continue to seek the approval from other men that he didn't get from his father?

The Score

If your man scores between 7 and 10 points, you have reason to be extremely concerned about his potential for maintaining a lasting heterosexual relationship. Short of a burning desire to deal with his latent tendencies, which may be helped by intensive therapy, there is little you can do to change him.

A score between 4 and 7 suggests that he may have conflicts in a heterosexual partnership. Before you become deeply involved with him, discuss those conflicts candidly and be certain that he has plans for working them out.

A score between 0 and 3 points is appropriate for an average male and does not indicate latent homosexuality.

Our deepest connections are those with men who remind us of our earliest love objects, often our fathers. Ideally, that person met your needs for love and nurturance and you will seek someone else to do the same. Too often, though, a woman makes her connections with a man who does not come through, just like the first man she loved. Unless she recognizes this pattern, she may blame her lover for her unhappiness and seek to change him rather than making a more appropriate choice.

Analyzing the Love Codes in a man's behavior before becoming deeply involved can help a woman avoid a serious mistake. In particular, scrutinize his actions before, during, and after sexual play, where important clues to his feelings about women are lodged.

CHAPTER · SIX

THE FRUIT
OF THE
FAMILY TREE

The family is the source of madness and the inspiration for genius. It is at the root of a man's capacity to love, the reason for his ability to feel joy, and the source of his deepest insecurity. Those things that make him angry and the accomplishments that make him proud are grounded in his upbringing. From a psychological vantage point, it is almost impossible to underestimate the impact of a man's family.

If you want to know what a man is like, take a look at his father. If you want to know how he relates to women, ask him how he feels about his mother. What sort of a parent will he be? Watch closely when he is interacting with his siblings!

Lifestyles: Not Necessarily Rich or Famous

GEOFFREY: ALL FOR ONE AND ONE FOR ALL

> Mara: One of the things that attracted me to Geoffrey was his wonderful family. Being with his parents was just like being with friends. We'd all go out to dinner together—sometimes

the four of us and sometimes his brother or sister and their dates, and we had a great time. We even took weekend trips and vacations together. I felt secure and loved by his parents in a way that I had never felt with my own family.

Geoffrey's primary family unit is the center of his social and emotional life, and any woman who becomes involved with him must be willing to become a part of it. Close-knit families invariably celebrate holidays together, plan big barbecues and picnics that all are expected to attend, and keep close tabs on everyone's whereabouts. A healthy family is not overbearing, however, but encourages individuality and makes plenty of room for new members.

Families that exclude outsiders, by contrast, tend to crush a man's ego and self-confidence. If he won't stick up for you or tends to ignore you when he is with his family, better think hard about where this relationship can go. But if he is mature enough to juggle family demands with his commitment to you, then you should give him the benefit of the doubt. Just don't try to force him to make a choice.

MITCHELL: DISTANT RELATIONS

Amanda: Mitchell and I have the ideal relationship with our parents. They live in California and we live in New York. We really enjoy our holiday visits—usually at Christmas and Easter—but after a few days in the confines of my parents' small town, I begin to feel strangled. The geographical distance between us gives us the freedom to live our own lives without interference from our parents. Mitchell and I depend on each other and on a handful of close friends for our emotional support.

Some children deliberately seek to separate themselves by moving far from the family home. Others may be separated from their families merely by circumstance and maintain involvement as best they can by regular visits, telephone calls, and correspondence.

Similarly, a "distant family" is not necessarily one that is far away. Children may live within a few miles of their families and even see them regularly, yet never leap the barrier that impedes emotional closeness. Men who were nurtured too little or protected too much had little positive experience with love in their formative childhood years. The result is difficulty developing emotionally binding relationships as an adult. Whether he continues to live in close proximity to his parents or moves far away, such men are constantly on guard against the possibility that you will seek to control them and will often reject your attempts at intimacy. They often crave close connections, however, and with your patience can learn to open themselves up.

FAMILY SHAME

Tara: Dan had postponed introducing me to his family for so long that I was convinced he was ashamed of me. It turned out, though, that he felt he really had to apologize for his parents. Visiting his family revealed a side of Dan that I had never seen before. Life in his suburban home was like a scene out of Archie Bunker, with Dan playing Meathead. Although I more fully understood why he sees his family so rarely, I don't think he has acknowledged how much he loses by neglecting his roots. His folks really are loving people, they just have a certain style that can be very grating.

Tara has correctly observed how important it is that Dan come to terms with his parents and learn to appreciate their worth. A man who is ashamed of his family carries a secret shame of himself because, like it or not, he is part of them. His harsh judgments on his parents are too easily warped into harsh judgments of himself and those close to him.

One element of maturity is the ability to make peace with your family. Dan must acknowledge his well of anger and accept his parents for better or worse before he will be able to create a happy family of his own.

DEREK: FAMILY COURT

Laurie: Derek prepared me for his family long before we were ever introduced. It will be like a trial before a jury, he said, and that turned out to be no exaggeration. I was grilled with questions and examined as though I were under a microscope. What did I do? What did my parents do? What was my relationship with Derek? How long had we known each other? How did we meet?

Derek was very supportive, which helped, but they certainly made it clear that I wasn't good enough for their son. What really irked me, though, was how they treated Derek. He wasn't good enough for them, either!

A judgmental family minimizes each of its members, ensuring that children grow up feeling unworthy and lacking in self-respect. Approach a relationship with such a man judiciously.

By preparing Laurie for meeting his parents, Derek proved that he had overcome the liabilities of his past and learned to accept their hostilities and dismiss their criticisms as irrelevant. He introduced her with pride and did what he could to shield her against their barbs, inquiries, and criticisms.

Unfortunately, many men aren't so mature. Instead, they are at once victim and persecutor; having been scrutinized so critically while growing up, they have never learned the virtues of forgiveness, acceptance, or patience. As a result, they apply their parents' standards to anyone they meet, especially women with whom they become involved.

CHARLIE: IT'S TRADITION

Beth: Charlie and I fit in so well with each others' families that our match feels as though it is meant to be. Our families are both very traditional and very conservative. Our fathers take charge of things outside of the home and our mothers run the household. Maybe I'm old-fashioned, but I think that's great. My parents have led a good life together and I'm looking forward to the same.

After a decade in which they felt increasingly pressured to compete in the job market, some women are rediscovering the option of being a mother and a homemaker. This does not mean that all achievements of the past decade need vanish. In any relationship based on mutual respect, no woman needs to be in an inferior or submissive role, even if she chooses to work in the home. What *is* important, however, is that expectations be clarified early in any relationship—and regularly reassessed as lifestyles change.

Beth was genuinely pleased at the role models of her past and perfectly willing to strive toward them. Other women, however, will express dismay to discover they have fallen into the same groove as their parents. And although many relationships begin with pledges of egalitarianism, old and familiar patterns often emerge. A man who grew up in a home in which his mother was chief cook and bottlewasher for his father may unconsciously expect you to treat him in the same way. Clear channels of communication early in the relationship are critical to prevent this from becoming a problem.

SCOTTY: BORN FREE

> Bonny: I never could figure out who did what in Scotty's family. His parents were really free spirits and they encouraged their children to be highly independent. Everyone was very creative but there wasn't much of a work ethic in the family. When money ran short, his father or mother would reluctantly get a steady job, then stick with it only until the bills were paid. I could see how this led to Scotty's happy-go-lucky

attitude about life and his own creative pursuits, but it just didn't jibe with my lifestyle. I need a lot more structure and security than he does.

A nontraditional family can spawn a free spirit—or a man who rebels by developing a rigid approach to life. The woman who becomes involved with an independent man inclined toward bohemianism must be prepared to sacrifice stability, predictability, and security for flexibility, freedom, and a communal life among kindred spirits. Bonny concluded that the tradeoff was not worth the risks; another woman, however, might welcome the opportunity to leave straitjacketed conventions to dabble in unknown realms.

The Divorced Home: For Better or Worse

Because some 30–50 percent of all marriages have ended in divorce, many men of marriageable age are the progeny of divorced parents. What are the effects of growing up in a divorced home?

- As with all traumatic situations in a child's life, a man can be strengthened by adversity and determined not to repeat his past. Or, he can feel defeated by the past and pessimistic about finding marital bliss.
- Studies show that boys in single-parent homes grow up faster and assume adult responsibilities earlier. He may grow

up to be rather serious and conservative, having foregone childish behavior at a young age, but he will not run from responsibility.

- Boys raised by single mothers are often particularly close to them and able to communicate openly and discuss their feelings. In a relationship, this translates into someone who understands the importance of intimate and emotional communication.

- Some men have a sense of emotional deprivation that makes them need a woman's intimacy. If a man blames his mother for his deprivation, however, he may carry the seeds of unresolved anger with him and frame situations in which a woman continually disappoints him.

- Children often blame themselves for their parents' divorce, which can create problems with self-esteem. In later relationships, this man will always apologize or take the blame for mishaps and you will find it difficult to convince him that he is worthy of your love.

- In a bitter divorce each parent may berate the other to their children. You must be very cautious about entering a relationship with a man who was exposed to this on a constant basis; he is inevitably filled with anger, usually toward both parents, and finds it difficult to trust anyone.

- Children who escape the most traumatic effects of divorce can emerge with a heightened awareness about the possibility of good relationships. When a divorce was amicable and both parties remain friendly, they can provide an atmo-

• sphere of love and security for their children that enables a man to accept the inevitability of change and approach love sensitively and sensibly.

The Heart of the Matter: His Parents

To understand a man's family Love Codes, the astute woman will look carefully at his maternal and paternal influences and notice how he interacts with his parents. A man is most likely to struggle with internal conflicts if the values of his parents clashed radically. When parents are compatible—or openly acknowledge differences between them and deal with them diplomatically—he is likely to be more confident about himself, although more set in his ways.

A man's relationships with his siblings can also be revealing because they set the pattern for future intimate relationships.

His Mother: The First Woman in His Life

The single most important question you can ask a man you meet is, "How do you feel about your mother?" Regardless of who you really are, a man will view you through the lens in which he sees his mother, and ultimately he will treat you the way he treats her.

If his answer is negative and you can still detect anger in his voice, approach this relationship with trepidation. A man's mother is the prototype for all his feelings about women, and if he is not comfortable with them, he is not emotionally capable of sustaining a mature relationship with another woman. A man who hates his mother unconsciously hates all women. Even if he also loves and needs a woman in his life, he will play out his anger about his past in your relationship and subject you to deep emotional pain.

Just as a man with negative feelings toward his mother will be critical and suspicious, a man with positive feelings accepts and appreciates the special qualities of a woman. If the bonds between a man and his mother are too tight, however, there may be no space in his life for a new emotional connection.

Observe not only what he says about his mother but how he relates to her. The old adage says that a man who is good to his mother will be good to his wife. Be on the lookout for answers to these questions:

• Does he offer her emotional support?

This is a man who can show love and compassion in response to a woman's needs without feeling obliged to agree with her at all times.

• Does he share news of his successes and failures with his mother right away?

A man who shares important news with his mother does so because he knows that she will be responsive and supportive to his parents. He will not bring unresolved conflicts or fears of intimacy into his adult relationships.

His Father: A Man's First Role Model

Most middle-class men in their late twenties and older grew up in traditional families in which the mother was the primary caretaker and the most important determinant of a man's feelings toward women. Nonetheless, a man's father serves as an important role model for the way in which a man will relate to a woman. Therefore, the second most important question to ask a man is: "How did your father treat your mother?"

Unless a man consciously rejects his father's approach to dealing with women, he is likely to repeat the same pattern. Thus, you will want to watch closely to see whether your man's father treats his wife with respect, compassion, sarcasm, or cruelty. Is she a confidante and a soul mate? How are responsibilities divided in the household? How does he view his wife's work? Has their relationship changed over the years?

Roots Unraveled: Parental Pairings and How They Shape a Man

How does the combination of different parental personalities affect a man's behavior in a relationship?

anything he says. A man who is accustomed to positive acceptance knows how to give of himself to other women.

• Is he proud to introduce you to his mother?

This is an indication of his respect both for her and for you and illustrates his ability to appreciate a woman's worth.

• How often does he speak or visit with his mother?

A man who enjoys his mother's company on a regular basis usually respects the value of a woman's companionship and has egalitarian feelings toward all women.

• When he describes how his mother raised him, is he understanding about components of his upbringing that he did not like?

Perfect parents, like perfect spouses, just don't exist. If a man accepts this about his mother, he will also be able to accept it about his wife. Such compassion indicates an ability to discuss problems openly and seek resolutions together.

• Does his personality remain the same when he is visiting his parents' home?

A man who has truly cut the apron strings and is comfortable about his own identity is neither intimidated nor rebellious with

Emotionally Aloof

A man who grows up in a home where both parents are cold and distant about expressing affection assumes this is the normal way of interacting. He is likely to focus more on objects and achievements than on people, because he does not readily make close connections.

Overprotective Mother, Absent Father

Lacking a strong role model, this man never gains sufficient confidence to assert his independence. He has learned, instead, that it is easier to allow women to take care of him.

Depressed Mother

When a mother is too depressed to extend herself for her children, they are certain to suffer emotional deprivation. The result is a man who denies himself pleasure, does not acknowledge his own needs, and can't shake his own sense of desperation.

A Nurturing Couple

The child of nurturing parents understands the importance of taking care of others. When a man is raised in a loving home, he usually learns to be confident and to develop skills that put others at their ease. Genuinely fond of other people, he is cooperative and trustworthy.

Indulgent Parents

Parents who are excessively indulgent of their children do them no real favors in the long run. Lacking encouragement to mature, a man's emotional development tends to be somewhat stunted.

Critical Mother, Passive Father

Because he has been made to feel humble and inadequate to women, the son of a critical mother usually suffers from lack of self-esteem. The problem is intensified by his father's inability to counteract her influence, which may leave him angry and depressed.

Demanding Mother, Underachieving Father

The offspring of such a couple feels compelled to achieve great things but lacks the confidence to do so. Pushed toward goals beyond his capacity or interest, yet lacking a role model to show him the path toward success, he faces contradictory pressures that often become impossible to handle.

Oh Brother (and Sister)

How does he relate to his siblings? And what does it mean for an intimate relationship?

- "Vincent became the head of the family at the age of 13 when his father died and he assumed serious adult responsibilities."

A man who assumes a lot of responsibility at an early age—perhaps by caring for an elderly parent or by taking charge of the family finances—will behave responsibly in a relationship. However, he is rather serious about life and often finds it difficult to set aside his role as an authority figure.

- "Chris hasn't talked to his brother in 15 years."

A man who is completely out of touch with his siblings demonstrates hostility and an unwillingness to forgive. In a relationship some of that buried anger is sure to surface.

- "Tim and his brother are best friends, live a few blocks from each other, and are in business together."

Men whose siblings are their best friends know how to maintain the strong emotional connections that you will appreciate in a lover.

- "Erroll visits his family only once a year. If he calls any other time, we know it is to ask for something."

A brother who calls his siblings only when he needs something from them does not understand that meaningful bonds are a two-way street. He'll expect a lot from you, too, but won't give much of himself.

- "Rudy is privy to all the family gossip but he never expresses an opinion or takes sides."

A man who remains neutral in all family squabbles, listening without comment to all sides of a dispute, tends to be emotionally detached. You may find it difficult to engage him in dialogue on subjects that he finds threatening, but his ability to see both sides of an issue qualifies him to mediate acceptable compromises.

Great Oaks from Little Acorns

Many experts say that half a child's learning takes place before the age of four. In addition to shaping his sense of security and his ability to form close bonds in those early years, a man's family influences his capacity for professional accomplishments later in life. The two case histories that follow illustrate how.

STEF: BORN TO WIN

> Irma: From the time we were teenagers, it was clear that Stef was destined for success. He was the oldest child and both his parents doted on him and pushed him to achieve. By the time he was 9 years old, he had created his own paper route; when he was 11 he hired his brothers to work for him so that he could branch out into bigger businesses, like delivering groceries and mowing lawns.

> I always admired Stef and as we got older, he began to pursue me with the ardor and determination I had seen him pour into his work. He showered me with phone calls and gifts until I finally relented and we began to date. He was the type of guy who knew how to get whatever he wanted; he just wouldn't take no for an answer.

Stef learned early in life that persistence is the key to success. From his youngest years he worked hard and constantly set new goals for himself. And he brought those same attributes into his adult relationships with women. Having known Stef from childhood, Irma was a step ahead of women who know nothing of a man's past. In particular, she knew that his parents' encouragement had given him a positive self-image, one of the important components of a mature emotional relationship.

Full speed ahead here. Stef has the determination, clarity of focus, and stick-to-itiveness that will carry a man far. Once he decided that Irma was the woman he wanted, he pursued her with the same vengeance that he pursued career success. Obviously Irma has no way of knowing whether Stef will continue to maintain interest once he wins her over. Nor does she know just how deeply involved she'll want to get with this man. But his persistence makes him a likely candidate for success, and it is certainly worth dating this man to see where it leads.

TOM: THE SEEDS OF DOUBT

> Victoria: Tom has a serious self-image problem. He's actually an accomplished musician and a good carpenter, but he can't shake himself free from his sense of failure. He does tend to leave projects unfinished sometimes, but I'm proud of him and very happy with our life together. I just wish he felt better about himself. The real problem is that he can't match the achievements of his older brother. Well, who can? John is an exceptional man—a superachiever and a nice guy besides! I think his parents played favorites with their sons when they were growing up together.

Unless parents strive to acknowledge the accomplishments of *all* their children, younger children may have difficulty competing with older siblings. The seeds of failure are planted in early childhood and often have little to do with actual performance. The anticipation of failure, like the expectation of success, can become a self-fulfilling prophecy. As an adult, a self-defined failure may give up instead of pursuing new opportunities, make faulty judgments, or take easy paths rather than challenging ones.

Move cautiously before becoming involved with such a man. You will have to spend a great deal of time bolstering his sagging spirits and conveying an optimistic outlook. It is also important to be strong and independent enough to separate your ego from his. Be appreciative if he has been made more sensitive and receptive to others because of his disappointments. Be suspect if he is embittered and blames others for his failures.

A man who feels good about his family life will seek to recreate it. The man who feels dissatisfied with his early experiences has a much more complex psychological challenge before him. Ideally, he will identify the gaps in his own upbringing and attempt to include what was lacking. Some men, though, are victims of their own fate, and unconsciously recreate early, unhappy experiences.

CHAPTER · SEVEN

THE SCRIPT THAT DIRECTS HIS EMOTIONAL SCENES

Women choose their men for a range of rational and not-so-rational reasons. Some make their selections purely on the basis of chemistry, others seek a man whose goals and values closely match their own. Whatever the motivation, his emotional profile is the personality factor that probably has the greatest effect on every aspect of your relationship.

Knowing what he will be like to live with at least gives you a fighting chance of deciding whether you really want to. Emotional stability, levels of tension and anxiety (and how he handles it), mood swings, and neurotic habits must all be assessed when considering the potential of a relationship. Keep in mind that it is as important to know thyself as to know your mate. Two moody people may be incompatible, for example, but a rock-steady man may be just the ticket for a woman whose emotions travel a roller-coaster path.

Although some men may be adept at masking their emotions, unconscious Emotional Love Codes cannot be readily hidden from an astute observer. In the next section, we'll run down a list of questions and answers to help you better understand what your man is all about.

What Makes Him Tick?
Self-Acceptance

- When others point out a fault, can he laugh and acknowledge the criticism? Or does he become upset and withdrawn?

Self-acceptance means acknowledging both one's attributes and failings. A man comfortable with himself is more accepting of others. Someone who is critical of himself also looks for faults in others.

Argument for Argument's Sake

- Does he start an argument just for the sake of the intellectual challenge?

Men who like to argue are usually energetic people who thrive on excitement. They may also be angry and manipulative, taking pleasure in asserting their intellectual superiority. There are only two ways to cope with a combative man: Either fight back or become his victim.

A Full Schedule

- Does he like to work hard and play hard or is he tentative about living life to the fullest?

A full and active life indicates a man who is self-confident, well-organized, goal-oriented, and energetic. Don't try to hold him down, because he'll resent you for it, but do take the opportunities that his rich life offers.

A man who is fearful confines his activities to familiar arenas. If you need more action, don't waste your energy trying to push this guy forward.

Bend, Don't Break

- Is he easily persuaded, rigid in his viewpoints, or willing to evaluate each situation individually?

Flexibility is the key to success in all relationships, but a man who discusses issues as they arise is infinitely more interesting than one who always accedes to your wishes without discussion.

At Ease

- Is he comfortable with strangers or constantly worried that things will sour in a new situation?

The man who trusts others and approaches new experiences optimistically adds depth to a meaningful relationship. Once he makes a commitment to you, he is open and perceptive enough to steer it in a positive direction.

Decisions, Decisions

- Does he have difficulty making decisions, such as choosing clothes, restaurants, vacation destinations?

A man who can't make up his mind lacks confidence in his own judgments and needs others to counsel him. But if you like to take charge, he might be just the ticket for you.

Don't Take It Personally

- When engaged in discussions, does he become embroiled in emotional attacks?

A man of intense emotions can be an amorous sexual partner but his inability to engage in a heated discussion without getting personal shows his lack of maturity. Don't despair, however. If he loves you enough, and you have the patience and fortitude to teach him to control his anger, he has the potential to change.

Giving Thanks

- Does he praise and thank you when you do even the smallest favor for him?

A man who is generous in offering praise and saying thanks is one who is generous in spirit and soul. He appreciates a woman and understands that love must be nurtured if it is to last.

Seeking a Scapegoat

- Does he complain that others take advantage of him or are out to ruin him?

By blaming others, this man reveals how sorry he feels for himself—but he does not take the responsibility to change his lot in life. Keep away—eventually he is certain to blame you for his misfortunes.

His State of Mind

Before probing the Love Codes revealed by certain personality traits, it is important to develop an overall sense of a man's emotional state. In the following quiz, you will select some of his most common moods.

Pick the six words that are most applicable to his usual emotional state:

1. Thrilled
2. Peaceful
3. Indifferent
4. Jittery
5. Agitated
6. Dejected
7. Exuberant
8. Patient
9. Self-absorbed
10. Stressed
11. Furious
12. Downcast
13. Buoyant
14. Tranquil
15. Blasé
16. Apprehensive
17. Hateful
18. Lethargic
19. Blissful
20. Satisfied
21. Submissive
22. Nervous
23. Resentful
24. Glum
25. Cheerful
26. Composed

27. Resigned

28. Anxious

29. Tense

30. Disheartened

List your six choices here:

The Score

Score as follows for each response:

5 points: Traits # 1, 7, 13, 19, 25.
4 points: Traits # 2, 8, 14, 20, 26.
3 points: Traits # 3, 9, 15, 21, 27.
2 points: Traits # 4, 10, 16, 22, 28.
1 point: Traits # 5, 11, 17, 23, 29.
0 points: Traits # 6, 12, 18, 24, 30.

[26–30 points]

This man has found the secret of a happy, fulfilling life and approaches each new day with renewed energy and enthusiasm. In a relationship you will find him eternally optimistic and supportive, and if his state of rapture is genuine—and if you can tolerate his endless good cheer—by all means consider getting involved. He'll brook no negativity from you, however, and if his optimism grates on your nerves, better make another choice rather than risk becoming resentful of him.

[21–25 points]

In general this man is quite satisfied with his life. Pleasant and levelheaded, he is not one to suffer pangs of self-doubt, depression, or unreasonable anxiety. Although he has a rather sentimental side, he is capable of communicating with you in an adult and rational way. Affectionate and kind, he rarely loses his temper, although he can when the provocation is great enough. In general, an ideal candidate for a relationship.

[16–20 points]

Although he is well-adjusted, this man feels that his accomplishments have fallen somewhat short of his goals. He expects a relationship to help him turn his life around by providing the stimulation and opportunities that he has been lacking. If you can shake him out of his complacency and tolerate the limits to his passionate side, you will find that he has the capacity to love with conviction.

[11–15 points]

This man focuses almost exclusively on his own troubles and has a knack for getting involved in the wrong things. Sometimes he is merely jumpy, other times he is almost frantic, and you may find his angry outbursts and moody introspection hard to take. No need to write him off entirely, however; if you can gain his trust and ease his fears, there may be a chance for a rewarding relationship.

[6–10 points]

Here is a hostile man who feels frustrated and powerless about many aspects of his life. Unfortunately, there is no way of gauging the remark or incident that is likely to send him on a tirade so you will often feel that you are walking on eggs when you are together. It doesn't take much to upset this guy—probably because he is so upset with himself. His rage sometimes emerges in the form of sarcastic remarks and constant putdowns of others, and the best way to deal with him is to steer clear.

[0–5 points]

It won't take long to realize how emotionally withdrawn this man really is. Humorless and despondent, he is indifferent to any sort of meaningful communication and won't respond to your efforts to lift him out of his depressed state. In time his grief may pass, but for the moment, he is too difficult to become involved with.

Emotional Personality Types

The extent of his insecurity, his preference for independent or close involvement, his readiness to anger, and his willingness to express feelings are all basic emotional states that have a significant impact on the course of a relationship. In the following pages we analyze some common emotional states and what they reveal about a man.

Insecurity Versus Security

Insecurity is a state of fear and doubt about one's ability to cope. Everyone feels insecure at some times and in particular arenas, such as at work or in relationships, and a little reassurance goes a long way. In the lives of some men, however, insecurity is so pervasive that it makes intimacy almost impossible.

In emotional interactions, men express their insecurities in many different ways—by being extremely loving and attentive, by being critical and aloof, or by acting passive and compliant. But the roots of the insecurity usually extend back to similar childhoods: Lacking approval for early accomplishments, they grow up feeling unworthy and inadequate.

Life with a secure man runs more smoothly and predictably. Because he is so self-confident, he usually demands less of your time and attention. But he may be less willing to make the same intense emotional commitment that a man with stronger needs will.

MILTON: SOCIAL INSECURITY

Sena: Milton is so insecure I don't dare look at another man when we are together. Even when we're at a party, I know I'll have a big fight on my hands when we get home if I talk to a strange man. That's why I try to maintain an independent social life and prefer going to parties alone.

Men like Milton are highly sensitive to perceived slights and constantly in need of reassurance. A woman with a strong independent streak may not respond well to his demands. On the other hand, a woman who tends to be insecure herself often prefers the safety of a man in whom she has complete faith.

If you become involved with an insecure man, be prepared to commit a lot of energy to soothing his ruffled feathers and establishing a bond of trust between you. Take heart though: Once that bond is established, this relationship has the potential to be deeply intimate and honest.

The Issue of Independence

A dependent man is one who leans on a woman for emotional support. Although his vulnerability sometimes seems excessive, a dependent personality is willing to make a commitment to a woman who treats him tenderly. Once he feels assured of your love, he has a lot to offer emotionally and if you thrive on close connections, this could be the guy for you.

An independent man, by contrast, will not lean on you but he also cannot be easily cajoled into keeping you company. He may be reluctant to spend a lot of time with your friends and family and won't attend cultural events or other activities with you unless he really enjoys them.

A CONSTANT COMPANION

> Maxine: In the beginning I thought it was so romantic that George wanted us to do everything together. After all, how many men will go shopping with a woman? Or consult her on

almost every decision? But after a while I began to feel suffocated. He wouldn't go anyplace without me—except work, of course, and even then he telephoned me constantly. Whenever I made my own plans, his resentment was palpable. I kept urging him to see his friends but outside of his weekly poker game, he wouldn't budge without me!

Independent women will find George's inability to function alone rather excessive; they prefer men who also value their own space. Other women crave a coupling as close as this one and will thrive on so much well-meant attention and affection.

Controlling

The impulse to control others has its roots in habit, a resistance to being controlled, and a man's slightly arrogant assumption that he knows what is best for the people he loves.

LIKE A BIRD IN A GILDED CAGE

Elly: I always liked a big, powerful man. When we began dating, Don made all the decisions for both of us and I felt well taken care of. Since we have been dating for a while, though, I have started to feel more like his prisoner. He makes all our social arrangements and insists on dropping me off and picking me up at work. He even tells me what clothes to wear and tries to give instructions to my hairdresser.

When I protest, he speaks genuinely about the depths of his love and says that he wants the best of everything for me. The dynamics of our relationship are making me crazy, yet I think it would be hard to find another man who would make me feel so safe and protected.

When they began dating, Elly was pleased to have Don assume the responsibility for her well-being, but inevitably began to feel stifled in a relationship that more closely resembles that of a parent and child than of two adult lovers. Although a woman who grew up without the certainty of parental love may be willing to sacrifice a degree of autonomy for security, Don's demands are extreme.

By denying Elly the right to her personal space, Don essentially tries to control her life. Unless she is willing to surrender her sense of self to Don, Elly will eventually have to gather the courage to set limits on his control. When she does, the depth of his commitment to her will be visible in his willingness to yield to her needs.

Angry

Some men habitually respond with anger to almost any conversation. This stems from a reservoir of anger and frustration that has accumulated over the years, especially during childhood. It is important that they vent their anger productively by channeling it into appropriate occupational and recreational pursuits.

NOT THE LAST ANGRY MAN

> Lydia: The first time I met Judd, he was reprimanding a man for smoking in the elevator. I was impressed with his courage and concern, but I've since learned that he is always ready to argue. He picks fights with me, quarrels with friends, and complains about trivial slights from waiters.

Lydia did not find it easy to remove herself from Judd's anger, but she was ultimately confronted by the need to detach herself from his irrational emotional responses or leave him altogether. Two types of women will survive in a relationship with a man who angers as readily as Judd: someone who has a calm disposition, a

strong ego, and is relatively free from anger herself, or a woman who needs to ventilate her own anger and thrives on the challenge of a heated debate.

Signs of a Simmering Volcano

Totally avoid the man whose anger manifests itself in physical violence, persistent emotional abuse, or antisocial behavior. There are no sterling qualities sufficient to compensate for the loss of your emotional or physical well-being. An irrationally violent response to provocation, or the suggestion that he has been involved in illegal activities or is a heavy drug user, are clear warnings to stay away.

Trust your instincts if you sense that something is amiss, because the clues that tip you off are not always obvious. Even casual remarks can indicate a deeper disturbance, especially if there is a pattern among them.

Here are some clues to emotional abuse:

- Hanging up the telephone in anger.
- Not returning phone calls.
- Berating you in public.
- Criticizing the way you dress or talk.
- Blaming you for mishaps.
- Making hurtful remarks to you or others, especially by deliberately mentioning sensitive topics.

- A sadistic sense of humor or practical jokes that are harmful or embarrassing.
- Cruelty in word or deed, especially to those who are vulnerable, such as animals, children, or the elderly.
- Striking or hitting you.

Here is evidence of antisocial behavior:

- Lying about where he spent an evening or who he was with.
- Bragging about escapades that never happened.
- Falsifying his family history, his professional credentials, or his accomplishments in order to impress you.
- Abusing service people, such as waiters and employees.
- Not tipping or failing to reward a person adequately for services rendered.
- Trying to get away with something—such as not repaying a loan, shoplifting, or not returning borrowed items.
- Turning an argument into a physical confrontation.
- Anger about perceived slights, such as having to wait for service or being jostled.

Compulsive

Conditioned to believe that spontaneity leads to error and impulsive action creates danger, a compulsive man's outlook on life tends to be somewhat rigid. Although he is usually aware of this trait, such a man cannot function effectively unless he is doing things his own way. Don't expect him to change significantly despite prodding from you.

SOL: NEAT AS A PIN

> Greta: Who says that a man can't be as neat as a woman? Disorder is Sol's nemesis. He is a little extreme but after all the sloppy men I have known, I am grateful to be involved with someone who cares about order and appearances. Although some of his habits drove me crazy at first, such as lining up his shoes and removing my clothes from behind the door, I am willing to accept his fastidiousness because he offers me so much in other realms of our relationship.

Although Greta did not share Sol's excessive sense of order, she was willing to compromise for the other rewards in their relationship. In particular, she was aware that compulsive men are usually stable and secure, and that certain compulsive habits, such as financial planning, social scheduling, and household organization contribute to success in our society.

But some women find a man like Sol, who needs to plan his life down to the last detail, too rigid for their tastes. His approach is particularly anathema to a freewheeling and spontaneous woman.

Nonemotional

The nonemotional man keeps his feelings under a tight lid, a trait that appeals to some women and drives others mad. As long as he can deal comfortably with your mood swings, the decision is yours as to whether your emotional makeup is compatible with his. The man to avoid is one who considers your displays of emotion unseemly and childish. He will be critical and undermine even your wish to talk about feelings.

MALCOLM: THE STOIC SUPPORTER

> Micki: In a given hour my emotions can roller coaster from tears to euphoria to anger. But Malcolm is a real stoic, the voice of reason in the midst of my hysteria. No matter how I react, he responds in a calm, cool, and collected manner that eventually relaxes me. My friends find him a bit cold, but that's just what I need—ice water on my hot head.

Although he is not particularly emotional himself, Malcolm accepts a woman's need to ventilate *her* emotions. He thus provided Micki the ballast that allowed her to explode without risk. Curiously, his nonemotional personality may also appeal to a woman inclined to suppress her own emotions.

Many women, however, will feel deprived by Malcolm's detached approach to his emotional reality, because the ability to share feelings is one of the basics of intimacy. Do not get involved with this man if you cannot function happily with someone who represses strong emotion. The tradeoff between open communication and a safe but superficial relationship will quickly become unacceptable to you.

What Symptoms Are Deadly to a Relationship?

To master the art of selecting the right lover, you must be able to extract larger meanings from small behavioral clues. The anecdotes that follow paint portraits of men who are exhibiting the classic signs of certain emotional types. At their best, these traits can be positive and productive. When they become excessive, however, they are magnified to a point at which they are out of control and self-destructive.

If you are to choose your man wisely, you'll need to understand the Love Codes behind his usual behavior and be able to distinguish healthy behavior from its extreme negative.

Is He Dissatisfied or Depressed?

Everyone feels a bit dissatisfied from time to time, but a depressed man carries that feeling to extremes. Someone who is merely dissatisfied accepts the need to make changes in his life and responds to the support and suggestions of others. A chronically depressed man, by contrast, lives as if a black cloud hangs constantly over his life.

Here is how you can recognize a hard-core depressive:

- He is never satisfied with himself or anyone around him.
- He always anticipates the worst and finds little joy in life.
- He has unrealistically high expectations that are doomed to be dashed.
- He blames others for his failures.

Although a compassionate woman can lend her support to a man who suffers from infrequent bouts of depression, relatively few women can be happy with someone who is chronically depressed, because the emotion is so contagious. Women who repeatedly become involved with depressed men are often depressed and angry themselves.

Is He Cautious or Anxious?

Caution and concern can be appropriate and useful responses to certain situations. Feeling tense about a new undertaking may prompt us to analyze it more carefully; for example, nervousness about a job interview may motivate us to prepare for it. Inappropriate or all-consuming anxiety, however, is usually a symptom of deep-seated insecurity and mistrust.

Because an anxious man does not feel confident that he can cope with events as they occur, he is uncomfortable with spontaneity and very resistant to change.

Here is how you can recognize a man who is afraid of his own shadow:

- He anticipates catastrophic outcomes from minor events.
- He is preoccupied with what others think of him.
- He looks back at an event and fears that he said or did the wrong thing.

A woman who becomes involved with him must be alert because anxiety can be chronic and all-pervasive. By focusing on the minute worries of daily life, he may deny deeper emotions. It will be difficult to get past his anxiety and his need for constant reassurance, and there may be few moments where you share good feelings together.

Is He Perceptive or Paranoid?

A perceptive man is one who can read the messages being relayed by subtle signals. Someone who combines natural astuteness with a generosity of spirit that encourages others to seek his advice is a rare and special friend indeed.

Unfortunately, hyperawareness in tandem with self-doubts can become warped and self-destructive. The perceptive man known for his willingness to help his friends can become the paranoiac who believes others are secretly plotting against him. Ironically, this assumption often stems from his own feelings of anger toward others.

Here is how you can identify a man whose judgment has been clouded by anxiety:

- He interprets completely innocuous statements as highly personal and negative judgments.
- He feels that the laughter and glances of others are directed toward him.
- He mistrusts the generosity of others, seeing it as an attempt to manipulate him.

No matter how perceptive he is about others, the paranoid man will have moments when he doesn't trust anyone—even you.

Is He an Optimist or a Pollyanna?

A man who has a positive outlook and expresses confidence in his ability to cope with the world can be a joyful companion. His eye is always upon the doughnut—never on the hole—and such enthusiasm can be contagious.

It is important to remember, however, the distinction between an optimist and a Pollyanna. Pollyannas operate on the basis of denial, ignoring all negative feelings in order to shield themselves from the intense sadness that underlies a happy-go-lucky demeanor.

Here's how you can recognize the man who carries good cheer to extremes:

- He never acknowledges negative feelings—yours, his, or those of anyone else.
- He is always prepared to find an excuse for other people, even when their behavior is clearly inappropriate.
- He refuses to anticipate problems—hence, he has no plans for a rainy day.
- He acknowledges neither the past nor the future but lives only in today's sunny present.

A man who blocks out deep emotions is uncomfortable in a close love relationship, because it is the willingness to share private feelings that provides the foundation for intimacy. Admittedly, many successful relationships are formed on the basis of common activities, with minimal emotional interaction. However, a woman who seeks psychological intimacy with her partner will feel unfulfilled with a man who cannot relate on that level.

Is He Health-Conscious or a Hypochondriac?

A man's concern about his health and well-being is admirable and indicates that he is also concerned about maintaining healthy relationships. When he focuses on every ache and pain in his body, however, it is an indication that he is using these concerns to express other feelings.

Watch for these signals of a real hypochondriac:

162 • Is He Mr. Right?

- He either cannot acknowledge, or doesn't realize, his true feelings, both physically or emotionally.
- He is preoccupied with his bodily functions and expresses his anxiety through them.
- He complains about imaginary ailments and exaggerates minor symptoms in order to attract attention and sympathy.
- His self-indulgence emerges only in his complaints of illness. In all other ways he appears to function as a responsible and caring adult.

A patient woman who correctly perceives his complaints as symptoms of anxiety and the need for attention can learn to love this man. Because there is a childlike quality to his emotional state, a hypochondriac is often receptive to the observations of others and will acknowledge his psychological condition, even if he doesn't change it.

Is He Energetic or Frenetic?

Whether they are driven by ambition, a passion for activity, or a commitment to a wide range of time-consuming interests, some men simply cannot keep still. There is a clear distinction between the merely energetic man, who is productive but emotionally mature, and the frenetic man, who keeps busy every single moment of the day in order to avoid facing his inner fears.

Here is what the man who is perpetually on the run does:

- He dissipates tension and controls strong emotions by focusing outward.
- He never does only one thing at a time.
- He overschedules himself and spreads himself thin.
- He never says no to a new idea or a new friend.
- He never gives all of himself to one project or to one person.

Although it can be stimulating to share your life with an active, even hyperactive man, he may have a tendency to ignore the woman he is involved with in his rush to fulfill other commitments. A man who operates at a level of high energy creates a mood of tension around him, and the woman he is with must be able to shield herself from his stress.

Is He a Charmer or a Manipulator?

The charmer frequently delights in pleasing others and thinks of himself as someone who brings joy into the lives of others. Footloose and fancy-free, he can be a delightful companion because he is not burdened by the responsibilities most conventional people assume in the course of their lives. However, he may also be an expert at manipulating others into taking care of him.

Here's how you can recognize the manipulative man:

- He feels that he is entitled to whatever he can get from other people.

- He's very generous when he's flush, but usually he is "waiting for a check" or has "'left his wallet at home."
- He is always boasting about some pie-in-the-sky deal but doesn't have any concrete plans for the future.
- He doesn't repay loans.

An otherwise serious and responsible woman may be attracted to a charmer because he enables her to act out her fantasies of rebellion. But be careful about overinvesting in this man—either emotionally or financially.

Is He Self-Indulgent or an Addict?

A man who knows how to relax and enjoy himself is a delightful and affectionate companion. A good bottle of wine and a hearty dinner, a few dollars won or lost on a football game, or several hours spent on the golf course are reasonable indulgences that provide a release from stress and tension.

It is when the indulgence becomes his central preoccupation—to the point of interfering with his personal life—that self-destructive addiction has developed.

Here are some of the traits of a man who travels over the border separating self-indulgence from addiction:

- He repeatedly and habitually engages in self-destructive acts.
- He uses addiction as an excuse to avoid strong emotions.
- He dreads emotional and personal confrontations.

- He is emotionally immature and dependent.
- He consistently opts for instant gratification rather than working toward longer-range goals.

Severe addictions can wreak havoc on the lives of anyone who becomes emotionally involved with them. Many different types of women have a pattern of repeated involvement with addicts—some see themselves as long-suffering martyrs, others are driven by the desire to dominate a weaker man. Whatever her personality type, the woman who repeatedly becomes involved with addictive personalities does so to avoid confronting emotional pressure.

Most emotional types are neither positive nor negative, although some types of men admittedly are more difficult to live with than others. The woman who thrives with a difficult man is someone who relishes challenge and risk and fears boredom. Not for her is the easygoing, stable relationship that can be deeply satisfying to a woman who thrives on consistency and predictability.

The better a woman understands her own personality type, the more likely she is to make a wise choice among the men who interest her. What makes you happy and secure? What kind of a trade-off are you willing to strike between independence and security? How do you react to a man who is not emotionally responsive? What balance between passivity and aggression is most suitable to your needs?

If you are honest with yourself as you consider these questions, your chances of striking the right match may increase dramatically.

CHAPTER · EIGHT

THE COST OF

HIS SUCCESS

In our society, money is not only our medium of exchange but a measure of status, achievement, and capability. As a result, both men and women tend to confuse success with earning capacity.

Actually, though, success is a subjective judgment, which is inextricably linked to an individual's personal priorities. Mother Teresa and Donald Trump are both successful—in very different ways, of course. Some women define a successful man as one who has attained the trappings of power and brings home a hefty paycheck, regardless of his emotional makeup. Others shrug off financial achievement in favor of personal autonomy or the pursuit of artistic endeavors. Regardless of her definition, every woman seeks a man whose success she can respect.

A successful man has a healthy outlook on life, generally appreciates his good fortune, and takes setbacks—financial and otherwise—in stride. As a result, he is accepting, rather than critical, of other people, and is ready to offer his help when he can. In a relationship, he will be generous not only with his credit card but with his time and emotional energy as well.

The man to avoid is the one whose greatest ambition in life is keeping his wallet full. Centuries ago a wise man asked: "What is a man profited, if he shall gain the whole world, and lose his own soul?" Unfortunately, many women choose men who don't know the answer to that question.

In this chapter we look at the trade-offs that are sometimes made between financial and relationship success and assess the Love Codes hidden in a man's approach to money.

His Glass Is Always Half Empty

No matter how they are praised, admired, and rewarded, some men never feel satisfied with their own achievements. Although such dissatisfaction can be a powerful driving force, it also indicates someone who is obsessed with his own performance. Beware the man who looks at others and feels that he can never match their accomplishments. As a lover, he will be convinced that you've been with better, sexier men in the past, and that he's not worthy of you.

Conversely, if he decides that he *is* worthy of your affections, then he'll conclude you're not good enough for him and lose interest. If he really interests you, try to make him aware of what he's doing, but don't expect miracles—he will have to confront his basic sense of inadequacy head-on if he is to change.

Through Rose-Colored Glasses

Equally unrealistic is the man guilty of the sin of pride, an arrogant braggart convinced that his accomplishments are unrivaled. Ultimately, he is sure to get his comeuppance, in part because he lacks the self-awareness to assess realistically his own strengths and weaknesses. In the meantime, steer clear. His false sense of superiority will come through loud and strong in an emotional relationship, where he will never admit to being wrong. He'll expect you to trust his judgment and let him have his own way.

Successful Predictions

Success and failure are more a matter of nurture than nature, but from childhood some people seem bred for success, whereas others appear destined for failure. Think back to your first-grade class and you will surely remember a range of personality types. Remember the aggressive kid who became the natural leader on the playground? And the teacher's pets, the shrinking violets, and the butts of other children's cruelty? How about those who stuck tenaciously to the task of solving a puzzle and others who gave up as soon as they became frustrated?

Obviously certain predictors of success are inherited. Good looks, high intelligence, and athletic ability are natural endowments that can be cultivated but not created from scratch. Still other traits—such as aggressiveness, determination, and patience—are a mixture of natural aptitude and learned ability. By looking closely at your man's personality traits and natural abilities, you can make a fairly accurate guess as to his likelihood of success—both personally and professionally.

Signs of Success

Regardless of their fields of endeavor, successful people usually have a number of traits in common. Among them:

- A sense of purpose.
- An ability to define achievable goals.
- Internal motivation and commitment to an end product.
- A willingness to take risks and bounce back from disappointment.
- A willingness to work hard.
- Patience to face and overcome obstacles.
- Tenaciousness and determination.
- The strength to seek advice and learn from others while ultimately keeping one's own counsel.
- Self-confidence.
- A sense of self-worth.

Signs of Failure

There are also common threads running through the personalities of those who regularly fail at what they undertake. Such men seldom have the capacity to maintain a mature relationship because they are intimidated by the responsibility involved.

Watch your man for signs of these handicaps:

- Failure to define his goals and the steps necessary to achieve them.
- The tendency to live in a fantasy world rather than to think realistically about his strengths and shortcomings.
- A low frustration tolerance that tends to make him give up easily or leave tasks unfinished.
- Laziness or distractibility.
- Lack of discipline or misplaced discipline (i.e., he tends to work hard in purposeless activities).
- Fear of success, perhaps because he feels that he does not deserve it.
- Fear of change, fear of competition, fear of failure.
- Arrogance or denial.
- Efforts to impress others by name dropping or the touting of past successes.
- Concealed or apparent nervousness.
- Sour grapes or negative attitude or excuses.
- Jealousy, envy, or put-down of others.
- A poor self-image or the lack of self-worth.

What Is His Potential for Success?

Answer each question with Yes, Sometimes, or No:

1. When he is wrongly criticized, does he stand his ground and defend his actions?

2. Does he have the ability to remain calm and collected in the face of opposition?

3. Before making a major decision, does he carefully weigh all its pros and cons?

4. Is he able to explain a task to others so that they can do the job he expects?

5. Does he maintain cordial friendships with business acquaintances?

6. Does he initiate projects without being asked?

7. Once he makes up his mind, having weighed all the factors, is it difficult to dissuade him from his decision?

8. Does he search carefully to find the person best qualified to do a job?

9. Will he defend a friend or employee who is being treated unfairly by others?

10. Is he appropriately cautious about investing money with casual acquaintances or those unknown to him?

11. When he is asked to do a time-consuming and tedious job, will he stick to it until it is completed?

12. When he fails, is he quick to pick himself up and try again?

The Score

5 points for every Yes; 3 points for Sometimes; 1 point for No.

[50–60 points]

Success is a function of perseverance, initiative, and loyalty, and this man ranks high in each one of these areas. Obviously self-confident and single-minded, he's got the characteristics of a high achiever and is likely to get what he wants from life.

This man is used to following his impulses and reaping the rewards. Nagging will get you nowhere with this guy; he has a strong streak of independence and won't be receptive to your efforts to change him. However, he will put the same effort into pursuing you as he does into pursuing success—if he decides you're the woman he wants.

[40–49 points]

Although this man also has a great capacity for success, he is just a touch less aggressive than the highest ranker and may not have the consuming determination necessary for outstanding achievement.

Conversely, there is more room for emotional involvement in his life. If your suggestions are carefully timed and tactfully phrased, he will listen gratefully and respond. Use your influence on him carefully, however—he tends to be a little cocky and if he perceives your efforts as an attempt to wrest control of the relationship, he is likely to turn cool.

[30–39 points]

This man's top priority is not professional success. He has some initiative and determination but doesn't possess much of the follow-through required for exceptional achievement. Don't expect him to rise to stratospheric heights. With a little encouragement, however, he will settle into a stable job in the middle ranks of his career and be moderately successful.

An emotionally satisfying relationship is quite possible with this man. He is not overly caught up in his work, yet has some of the attributes desirable in an intimate relationship. Check his answers on questions 3, 4, 5, 8, 9, 10, and 12. If the answers are "yes," full speed ahead for the woman who does not overrate the value of professional accomplishments.

[19–29 points]

It is doubtful that this man will ever achieve major successes. Despite his good intentions, he lacks the strength of purpose to make his visions a reality. Timid about his convictions, he will probably opt to settle into a steady, salaried position that doesn't demand much energy from him. Reconsider if your dreams are ambitious ones. But if you are as laid-back and easygoing as he is, and share his limited goals, then proceed forward.

[Below 19 points]

Proceed with caution, because this is a very poor prospect. He is programmed to fail at almost anything he tries. Unless you relish the idea of constantly picking him up and brushing him off—only to see him fall right back down again—it's probably best to seek a more suitable candidate.

Balancing Emotional and Financial Success

Lucky is the woman who finds a man whose success has not been obtained at high emotional cost. Although sound finances and emotional maturity are far from incompatible, some men don't seem able to put energy into obtaining both.

Alas, when one is sacrificed at the expense of the other, there are usually negative personal and professional consequences. Sometimes the single-minded pursuit of money enables a man to hide from his emotions. Other times his efforts to attain emotional maturity seem to cripple his commitment to work.

Financial Successes—Emotional Failures

The 1980s seem to have spawned a generation of professional workaholics for whom career success is an overwhelmingly important source of satisfaction. But men who focus single-mindedly on career achievements are often uncomfortable in emotionally charged interpersonal relationships. Rather than admit to being vulnerable, they concentrate their energies on the external manifestations of success. The self-image problems of a man who confuses net worth with self-worth usually result in vapid love relationships.

Here are the problems you can expect with the man who is a financial success but an emotional failure:

- He may be a good provider but he'll tolerate few emotional demands.
- He will not be available to share family responsibilities and problems.
- Although he is committed to your relationship, he will insist on maintaining an uncomfortably high degree of independence.

Some of the most sought-after men are workaholics. Why do women pursue them with such interest? Partly because they are at the pinnacle of their success and convey enthusiasm not only

about their work, but about life itself. And partly because their personal and financial power is a very appealing attribute.

Only a woman who has strong and independent interests of her own is likely to find a workaholic a very desirable candidate for love. The following portraits paint two different types of workaholics.

PIERRE: ALL WORK AND NO PLAY

> Andrea: Pierre and I dated for three years before I discovered how limited our relationship was. I know that sounds crazy, but we had always stressed the importance of maintaining independent lives. Between building my own career, socializing, and trying to stay fit, I was really very busy and quite satisfied. Only when he started pressuring me to get married did I realize how far apart we had grown.
>
> The reason was obvious. Pierre worked all the time. He ran his own business and never found time to take a vacation or even a long weekend away. At night he was too tired for sex, and in the morning he was too tired to talk (and vice versa). I think he wanted to get married simply because it was convenient; certainly not because he was willing to put renewed energy into our stale relationship.

Extreme caution here. A workaholic like Pierre is essentially a one-dimensional man who pours all of his passion into work and retains none of it for life's other pleasures. His interest in marriage did not derive from genuine devotion to Andrea but from a sense that marriage was the appropriate and proper course for a man in his position.

The fault in this situation does not lie exclusively with Pierre, however. For three years Andrea allowed their relationship to drag on and never stepped back from her own busy life to acknowledge its limitations to try to change the situation. A healthy relationship requires that both parties keep their eye on its evolution and communicate with each other when problems begin to arise. Yet not all communication is what it appears to be.

BULLISH ON BUSINESS

Bridget: Sam called me at work several times a day to talk endlessly about his business dealings. At first this made me feel very important in his life, but eventually I realized how limited the range of his interests was. He never asked about me and we never tackled emotional issues unless I raised them. In fact, business and money were the only subjects that Sam really cared about.

In the beginning of a relationship, it is easy to mistake conversation about business for meaningful communication. This is a time when you are filled with curiosity about his life. Perhaps you feel flattered when he takes you into his confidence and see it as a reflection of his interest in you. But Bridget initially failed to see that Sam's conversation did not represent true *communication*. In its ideal form, a shared dialogue means an exchange of interests and feelings; at least some of the time, those feelings should be personal and focused on the two of you.

How to Add Emotional Fabric to Material Fiber

Fortunately, there is cause for hope. All financially successful men are *not* emotional adolescents. And some who are, are willing to change.

One method is to shower a man with love and attention. Although most of his passion may be poured into bank statements and stock investments, an open man can be very susceptible to an adoring woman willing to help him cultivate his emotional side. This is particularly true of an older man. Having already established himself professionally and attained a degree of financial independence, he may at last be ready for the challenge of an intimate relationship.

Emotional Success—Financial Failure

Some men are financial failures because:

- They are intimidated by the need to compete with other men.
- They fear the risk of failure.
- They unconsciously believe themselves unworthy of it.
- They place their artistic visions or personal preferences above the drive to make money.

Many men who refuse to conform to society's traditional expectations cultivate their emotional needs to the exclusion of their professional ones. A woman's ability to be happy with such a man depends mostly on her personal priorities and financial needs.

CAN THERE BE CAKE WHEN THERE IS NO BREAD?

> Renee: Andy is the sweetest, most loving, and generous man I've ever met, but he has absolutely no interest in making money or improving his lifestyle. I respect his determination to succeed as an actor, but in his mid-thirties I think he needs to be more realistic about the odds and seek a different path. He's highly disciplined about his acting classes and rehearsals, and thoroughly lazy about seeking better-paid work. When funds get tight, he'll take the first odd job that comes along, but he'll quit in a minute if an acting opportunity comes up, even if it pays absolutely nothing.

There is an element of selfishness and a hint of adolescent behavior in a man too stubborn to change for the good of a relationship. A man who scoffs at the importance of material possessions often has an unrealistic attitude toward life and relies on others to take care of him.

The key to a relationship with a man unable to earn a decent income is his lover's ability to adjust to the situation. A woman who is willing to live on a limited income or assume breadwinning responsibilities in return for emotional closeness and personal power, could find this relationship eminently satisfying. After all, how many of us crave a man who is happy, faithful, emotionally involved, and supportive?

But this is not the right man for a woman who needs to be financially secure or is interested in the high achiever willing to play by the rules for success.

Making Sense of His Dollars

Money is frequently cited as the primary source of marital discord. Because of its importance in our society, it has a value that far transcends its worth as a medium of exchange, becoming instead the means by which we express ourselves and communicate with others. It reflects our feelings of self-worth, love, and power.

The way a man builds his personal assets often matches the evolution of emotions. Some men spend cautiously and place most of their assets in secure, steady investments, such as government bonds and CDs. Others live for the moment, and when they do invest, gamble on stocks and commodities, hoping for greater gains.

What Kind of Investment Will He Make in Your Relationship?

The ways in which a man invests his money tell you the kinds of risks he's willing to take in life and how much effort he will put into a relationship.

1. Government Bonds and CDs

This man does not like to take risks and prefers the security of limited goals. If he likes you, he will be willing to commit to a relationship readily and remain satisfied and loyal.

2. Day-to-Day Savings and Money Market

Like his assets, this man likes to keep his relationships fluid. He wants to have control over any eventualities that may arise and often continues to seek other women while dating one just in case a better opportunity comes along.

3. Stocks and Commodities

Here's a gambler who trusts his instincts and thrives on the excitement of new possibilities. He's the kind of guy who'll jump into a relationship, but is open to trading if he thinks the growth potential is limited here.

Understanding the Love Codes behind a man's financial approach will give you a deeper understanding of his prospects as a lifetime partner.

AUDITING A RELATIONSHIP

> Fran: Although Gerald was earning tons of money, and investing it wisely, he still kept a record of every penny he spent. He resented the cost of entertaining, never took vacations, and resisted buying new clothes. He made me account for every cent I spent. And he was stingy in other ways, too—our lovemaking was bland, devoid of any real intensity or intimacy.

Gerald is a poignant example of why money can't buy happiness. Although he acquires money to feel secure, the fear of losing it actually intensifies his insecurity. His tension and rigid behavior make him incapable of meaningful love.

Is This Man a Good Love Risk?

1. If he needs to purchase a particular item does he wait for it to go on sale?
   a. Usually.
   b. No.
   c. Yes.

2. Does he overspend in order to impress other people?
   a. No.
   b. Yes.
   c. Occasionally.

3. If he has a limited clothing budget, does he:
   a. Buy one expensive suit.
   b. Purchase several inexpensive garments.
   c. Repair and update the apparel he already owns.

4. What does he do with his old newspapers and magazines?
   a. Saves them in piles all over his home.
   b. Throws them out every day.
   c. Keeps a few of the ones that contain important articles.

186 • Is He Mr. Right?

5. *When using toothpaste or paper towels, does he:*
   a. Use more than he actually has to?
   b. Use less than he actually should?
   c. Use about the right amount?

6. *When it comes to items that spoil, such as fruits, vegetables, or milk, does he:*
   a. Tend to buy more than he needs?
   b. Tend to buy less than he needs?
   c. Buy just the right amount?

7. *Does he turn off the lights and appliances in his home or apartment when they are not being used?*
   a. Always.
   b. Sometimes.
   c. Never.

8. *What does he do at a restaurant when there is too much food to eat?*
   a. Asks for a doggie bag.
   b. Lets the food be cleared away.
   c. Attempts to finish everything on his plate.

9. *When paying for a meal in a restaurant, or buying clothes or other items, will he:*
   a. Always use a credit card?
   b. Sometimes use a credit card?
   c. Rely strictly on cash?

10. *If he drives a car, is the vehicle:*
    a. Expensive and beyond his means?
    b. A little too small and economical for his lifestyle?
    c. One that truly reflects his income?

The Score

Add together the points scored for each question to get the total score.

1. a/4 b/2 c/6
2. a/6 b/2 c/4
3. a/2 b/4 c/6
4. a/6 b/2 c/4
5. a/2 b/6 c/4
6. a/2 b/6 c/4
7. a/6 b/4 c/2
8. a/4 b/2 c/6
9. a/2 b/4 c/6
10. a/2 b/6 c/4

[50–60 points]

This man is a cautious, practical individual who is not prone to taking financial risks. He is more likely to put his money into CDs and mutual funds than to risk them in speculative stocks. Conservative and responsible, only the security of a solid economic base makes him feel comfortable.

His choice in a partner is similarly based on practical considerations. Don't expect a whirlwind romance or intense passion from him. This man is searching for a woman whose goals and values are compatible with his own; when he finds her, he will treat her kindly and well. He is rigid in his ways, however, and does not take kindly to criticism, so don't expect impractical gifts from him.

[40–49 points]

Slightly more carefree, this man takes a few well-informed risks now and then but never goes too far out on a financial limb. Although he may put a small amount of his funds into questionable investments, the bulk of his assets remain secure in low-risk, low-gain accounts.

Surprises aren't welcomed by this man. He can accept, even appreciate, a woman with a bit of charming idiosyncrasy, but he is basically serious about proper behavior and generally plays by the rules. He is a good prospect if you value responsibility without excessive frills.

[29–39 points]

This score suggests a man who is frugal one day, then swept away by his desires the next. He can be very conservative and then, suddenly, succumb to an impulsive urge to buy an extravagant possession. In general, he is financially responsible, but he has been known to undo years of good investment through one high-risk adventure. Some men in this category have gambling instincts that can lead them into serious difficulties if they let down their guard.

If you meet this man during one of his impulsive moments, he may sweep you off your feet. But momentary exhilaration can turn into terrifying insecurity if you do not have ample financial and emotional resources of your own. Better be sure that he's willing to allow you to handle the family finances before trusting your fate to him.

[20–29 points]

This guy is extravagant to the point of wastefulness. He lives for the moment because no one ever schooled him in the necessity of saving for a rainy day. His boisterous and lackadaisical attitude toward money often extends to his relationships. He's rather careless with his affections and a bit insensitive in showing his appreciation of your efforts.

This guy's wastefulness and big-spender mentality is a source of irritation to many women, especially when he starts spending their money. If he's got plenty of the green stuff, sit back and enjoy it while it lasts. Watch out, though, if he is living beyond his means. As soon as he reaches his credit card limits, he'll be looking to you when the tab arrives.

From the earliest moments of a relationship, pay close attention to the way he talks about success and money. Do finances consume only a reasonable proportion of his attention? Does he successfully balance the time he devotes to money-making enterprises with the energy he puts into love relationships? Are his fiscal investments sound ones or based on get-rich-quick schemes?

Unless you can answer yes to all three questions, better keep a close watch on this man. If financial success is your motivation for pursuing a relationship, then full speed ahead. But don't expect much emotional interaction. Keep your distance if money is not your main priority.